Teachings of Jesus

Teachings of Jesus

Alicia Batten

NOVALIS

Cover design: Allegro168.inc

Layout: Audrey Wells

Business Office:
Novalis
49 Front Street East, 2nd Floor
Toronto, Ontario, Canada
M5E 1B3

Phone: 1-800-387-7164
Fax: 1-800-204-4140
E-mail: cservice@novalis-inc.com

www.novalis.ca

Library and Archives Canada Cataloguing in Publication

Batten, Alicia
    Teachings of Jesus / Alicia Batten.

ISBN 2-89507-596-4

    1. Jesus Christ–Teachings. 2. Bible. N.T. Gospels–Quotations.
    I. Title.

BS2415.B37 2005   232.9'54   C2005-904154-4

Printed in Canada.

We acknowledge the financial support of the Government of Canada through the Book Publishing Industry Development Program (BPIDP) for our publishing activities.

5 4 3 2 1   09 08 07 06 05

NOVALIS

To Aileen and Richard Batten,
with love

Acknowledgments

I would like to thank John L. McLaughlin for inviting me to write the fourth volume of this series, for providing editorial suggestions, and for producing the Preface to this book. Special thanks are also due to Kevin Burns and Anne Louise Mahoney, both of Novalis, for their generosity and careful reading of the text. As I worked on the manuscript, various members of the Religion Department at Pacific Lutheran University upheld their reputations as encouraging and stimulating colleagues. My spouse, Terry Rothwell, continued to be a helpful and challenging conversation partner as I shared some of my ideas with him. Finally, I am grateful to my parents, Aileen and Richard Batten, for their interest and support over the years. I dedicate this book to them.

Alicia Batten

Contents

Preface

Teachings of Jesus is the fourth volume in the Jesus Speaks Today series. This series of books takes the Gospels seriously as God's Word – addressed not only to the early Christians, for whom they were originally written, but also to us today. The four Gospel writers wrote slightly different versions of Jesus' life, death and resurrection because they were concerned with the significance of Jesus for their individual communities. Each was trying to answer the question "What does Jesus' ministry mean for us?" The Jesus Speaks Today series seeks to do the same for modern readers.

Each book in the series reflects upon a different aspect of Jesus' earthly ministry 2000 years ago in order to illustrate the continuing relevance for our contemporary world. In *The Questions of Jesus* (2002), I examined some of the many questions Jesus asked in the Gospels. Discussing how the original audience would have understood them served as a basis for considering the way we can understand and respond to those questions today. Richard Ascough did the same in *Miracles of Jesus* (2003), situating the miracles within the understanding of sickness and healing that Jesus shared with his contemporaries and then applying the results to our modern time. In *Parables of Jesus* (2004), I looked at a number of Jesus' parables, reflecting on what they meant for a first-century audience in order to relate that meaning to a 21st-century audience.

Following the pattern of those three volumes, Alicia Batten focuses on Jesus' teachings with the same question in mind: How is this relevant for believers today? In order to answer that question she considers Jesus' teachings within both the context of the Gospels themselves as well as their first-century Mediterranean context. She begins by examining the role of a teacher not just in ancient Israel but also in the larger Greco-Roman Empire. Jesus' audience was familiar with the content and style of both Jewish and Greek teachers, and therefore would have heard and responded to his teachings in light of that experience.

In each chapter of this book, Batten discusses a different teaching in the light of this understanding of Jesus' ministry in the ancient world. As a result, she is able to provide significant insight into what the teaching meant for those who heard or read it for the first time. She then reflects on the sayings in terms of their relevance for us today. In this way Jesus' teachings take on fuller meaning for the faith life of modern believers; indeed, Batten better enables us to experience Jesus' words as a challenge to our own lives, just as they were to his first listeners.

I'd like to explain some of the words and phrases used in this book. First, traditional terminology for the two main divisions of the Bible is problematic and has implications for how one interprets both of those sections. "Old Testament" connotes "antiquated," "outdated" and even "replaced" for some. "Hebrew Bible" is popular in many circles, but designating the material by its (primary) language of composition does not take into account those parts of Daniel and Ezra that were written in Aramaic or the extensive scholarly use of ancient versions in other languages, to say nothing of the second part of the Bible, which still tends to be called the "New Testament." "Hebrew Bible" also does not incorporate the deutero-canonical books, some written exclusively in Greek, which Roman Catholics and Eastern Orthodox Christians consider scriptural but Protestants and Jews do not. Similarly, "Jewish Bible/Scripture" is inadequate for Christians in general, for whom the first part of the Bible is also part of their Scriptures. As a compromise, the terms First Testament and Second Testament are used in this book for the two main divisions of the biblical literature.

Second, in the following pages the phrase "Synoptic Gospels" is used in reference to the Gospels of Matthew, Mark and Luke. These three are called "synoptic" because, in contrast to the Fourth Gospel (John), their presentation of Jesus can be seen (-*optic*) together (*syn*-). Because many similarities exist between them, they can be arranged in three parallel columns (various editions of such a synopsis have been published). Once they are viewed side by side in this way it becomes clear that Matthew, Mark and Luke describe the same basic events from the life of Jesus in roughly the same order and often with the exact same words. This suggests that there is a literary relationship among those three Gospels, namely that two of the authors have copied significant portions from one or two of the others. The most commonly accepted solution to this "synoptic problem" is that Matthew and Luke, working independently of each other, followed the narrative outline and content of Mark, but also supplemented him with material taken from a collection of Jesus' sayings. This second source is designated with the letter "Q," from the German word *Quelle*, which simply means "source."

Batten's treatment of Jesus' teachings is consistent with this solution. Although each chapter focuses on a saying from a specific Gospel, she frequently illustrates the distinctiveness of how that Gospel uses the saying by considering how Matthew or Luke adapted Mark's earlier formulation of a teaching in order to reflect specific concerns.

Third, "the LORD" is used in place of the name of the God of Israel. Even though the name is present in the ancient Hebrew manuscripts of the First Testament, a growing sense of the sacredness of both God and God's name, plus a concern that one might inadvertently take God's name in vain, meant that people eventually stopped pronouncing the name that was written. Instead, to this day observant Jews substitute the term *ădōnāy*, which means "my Lord," wherever the name itself appears. In keeping with this practice, "the LORD" is used in place of the divine name, but it is written in capital letters to signify that it refers to God's name and not just the generic word "lord."

Finally, the abbreviations BCE and CE are used. These stand for "Before the Common Era" and "Common Era." They cover the same period as BC ("Before Christ") and AD ("Anno Domini" = "The Year of the Lord"), but the first set of abbreviations is more commonly used by biblical scholars.

Each of the following chapters begins with a reference indicating where the specific teaching to be discussed can be found in one of the Gospels. Reading about the Bible should not take the place of reading the Bible itself, so read each passage before you read the chapter. This book uses the New Revised Standard Version when quoting from the Bible, but any competent modern translation will do. Differences in wording among translations are the result of the different translators' choices concerning how to render a word that has more than one nuance. Such matters should not interfere with letting the biblical texts come alive for you today, which is the purpose of this book.

To that end, open your heart to hear God speak through these reflections on God's own word.

John L. McLaughlin
Series Editor
Faculty of Theology
University of St. Michael's College
Toronto, Ontario
April 4, 2005

1

Jesus the Teacher

Throughout the gospels, Jesus is called *rabbi* or *rabbouni*. These terms are two forms of the word for "sir" or "master" in Aramaic, a Semitic language related to Hebrew and Arabic that was spoken by many people in first-century Palestine. Sometimes this word was used to describe a teacher of the Jewish Law; the author of the Gospel of John provides a translation, *didaskalos*, which means "teacher" in Greek. The Gospel of Mark refers to Jesus as *rabbi* or *didaskalos* on several occasions. Thus there can be no doubt that one way Jesus was remembered, early on, was as a teacher. But what did first-century Jews, living in the region known as Palestine, understand a teacher to be? And given the roles of teachers in antiquity, what sort of teacher was Jesus?

Let us begin by examining the context in which Jesus lived. Jesus was born, lived and died a Jew in a region that had been conquered by one empire after another for about six hundred years (except for one period that lasted for less than a century). At one point, Alexander the Great led his military campaigns throughout the region and, as a result, spread the language and culture of Greece, a process known as Hellenization. By the first century CE, Palestine had come under Roman control and was ruled by the Romans indirectly through client kings. Herod the Great was one such king. Because of his oppressive rule and heavy taxation policies, many living in Palestine hated him. His reign came to an end during Jesus' infancy. His son Herod Antipas was installed by Rome to rule the region of Galilee, where the village of Nazareth was located. Judea, the province to the south, was taken over by Archelaus, another son of Herod the Great, but he was an incompetent ruler whom the Romans replaced by a governor. By 26 CE (or perhaps earlier), the person occupying this position was a man named Pontius Pilate.

Attention to these political dimensions of Jesus' context is essential to understanding the memory of him as a teacher, and I will return to them occasionally as we work through some of the teachings. Moreover, although Jesus was Jewish, this history reveals that he lived in an area that was familiar with Greek language, culture and ideas. Jews were not the only inhabitants of Palestine: a variety of peoples, many of whom spoke Greek (including Greek-speaking Jews), lived there. Over time, as is usually the case when people from diverse religions, languages and traditions live together, these cultures came to influence one another. Thus, in order to understand the role of a teacher in such a context, one must examine not only Jewish traditions, but also those of the Greek and Roman world.

But first, it must be noted that education in antiquity took place in numerous ways, including through the family, religious groups and a variety of "schools." Within the Roman Empire, only a small section of the population learned to read and write. Those who attended formal schools were a minority. But in both Jewish and Greek contexts, other educational settings existed. These were often formed when a teacher attracted a group of disciples. Also, sectarian communities, such as the Jews who lived at Qumran, near the Dead Sea, developed their own educational practices.

During the first century, Jewish teachers were associated with teaching wisdom and interpreting Torah. (By "wisdom" I mean both the pursuit of knowledge about the world and how it works, as well as what it means to be human.) Generally, such teachers were highly revered. Wisdom literature reflects upon how one should act in the world, both towards other human beings and in response to the creator. Texts in the First Testament such as Proverbs, Sirach and Ecclesiastes, among others, are commonly understood as wisdom texts. There are no Second Testament texts that are purely wisdom teachings (although wisdom teachings pervade the Letter of James), but the various writings do pick up on the wisdom tradition, and many understand Jesus to be a wisdom teacher or sage. The rabbis continued this tradition later on, often using parables as a means of conveying wisdom in short narrative form. Rabbis also upheld the responsibility for interpreting Torah in new contexts, and many stories that have been preserved contain heated discussions of how certain biblical passages are to apply to specific situations. In some rabbinic texts that emerged after Jesus, moreover, the student's teacher has a higher status than the student's father.

It was less common in Judaism, however, for teachers to gather students or disciples around them, as Jesus does in the gospels. Rather, in Judaism the potential student would seek out the teacher and request to become part of his circle of disciples. Greek writings, however, contain examples of teachers gathering followers to them and then travelling around, proclaiming their message (which often consisted of social critique) to those who would listen. Within the last fifty years, historical Jesus scholars have noticed to what extent sayings and stories associated with Jesus parallel these Greek traditions. Given the Hellenization of Palestine, it is not unrealistic to think that Jesus would have encountered these sorts of philosophical teachers. In some texts that have survived, such teachers are respected for their wisdom and bravery, while in others they are criticized.

As we examine some of the teachings of Jesus, therefore, I will occasionally refer to other texts, Jewish and Greek, which are comparable to the teaching under discussion and which will provide a broader context for understanding the teaching. I will discuss a variety of teachings from each of the four gospels in the Second Testament, so that the reader will gain a sense of how the character of teachings attributed to Jesus varies somewhat according to the emphases of each gospel writer. My aim is to equip the reader with both a sense of how some of the teachings attributed to Jesus would have been understood in the first century and how, over two thousand years later, these teachings continue to be relevant.

Many of us can name a teacher whose influence prompted us to re-evaluate our goals or opened the door to possibilities that we had never imagined. Jesus, a great teacher, opens up new possibilities. His teachings are not always crystal clear, but they do offer a different vision, often a radical one, of life and of relationship to the divine. I hope that while reading these pages, you will reflect upon the responsibility teachers bear to prod us to think more deeply, even when such thinking is difficult and uncomfortable.

Although Jesus' teachings do offer insights for us today, I do not think he wanted his followers to follow them slavishly, but rather to think about them for themselves. Thus, while one aim of this book is to provide opportunities for reflecting on the teachings of Jesus, I also hope that it will pave the way for creative and focused thinking on how to live them out in our complicated, broken, yet precious world.

2

Physicians for the Sick

"Those who are well have
no need of a physician,
but those who are sick."
Mark 2:17

Just as is the case in many parts of the world today, there were no antibiotics or ambulances in antiquity. But people at that time did have the means to deal with sickness and disease. People would sleep in temples to healing gods in the hope of being cured; military installations had hospital-like quarters for the wounded and sick; the Romans built therapeutic baths; and many people travelled to natural water sources in search of relief from their ailments. Some physicians and surgeons were part of wealthy households (they were often slaves), while others travelled around setting up small clinics in the marketplaces of cities and towns. There was no formal certification process for doctors, however, and thus the chief problem for many was whether the physician in question was a charlatan. Doctors had to build solid reputations for themselves.

Even with a good physician and effective treatments, however, people still died of maladies that we in Western, developed countries would consider treatable or curable. Tooth abscesses, wounds that became infected, and many types of disease were common causes of death. In fact, those who lived past age thirty were seen to be very fortunate. Disease often had a social function as well. For example, people who had a visible skin condition, such as psoriasis, would not only suffer physical discomfort, but could also be easily identified by the community as a source of impurity. The afflicted person would thus be marginalized and suffer social, emotional and economic consequences as well.

In Mark 2:17 we encounter a brief proverb, or wisdom saying, that is also found in ancient secular writings. Jesus appears to share the common-sense view that it is simply those who are sick who need a doctor. The proverb testifies to Jesus' general interest in the welfare of the sick, which is evident in other things he says and in the healing miracles he performs.

Let's look at the context of this proverb in the Gospel of Mark. Jesus makes this statement in response to some Pharisees who question his dining with tax collectors and sinners. Jesus utters the teaching, then adds, "I have come to call not the righteous but sinners." Thus the Gospel of Mark has taken an independent proverb, placed it within a controversial discussion about eating with sinners, and effectively interpreted it to be about how Jesus calls sinners and not the righteous. We will see that the gospel writers often use this technique when reporting the sayings of Jesus, for just as we struggle to interpret Jesus' teachings for today, they struggled to interpret them for their own communities. The communities that the gospel authors wrote for were fragile, full of questions about who Jesus was, and in need of hope and guidance. The gospel writers, who had received sayings and stories of Jesus that were passed down to them in both oral and written forms, wove these into their gospels. At the same time, like pastors who seek to guide their congregations, each interpreted the life and ministry of Jesus to make it meaningful to their community.

It is also worthwhile to attempt to understand Jesus' teachings on their own, even though it is difficult to know when and where he made such statements. Here, Jesus probably intends the proverb to be taken literally. His point is that sick people, not healthy ones, need a physician. In antiquity, those who were poor, undernourished, and living in dangerous and difficult conditions were more likely to be sick than the rich. Disease could strike anyone, but the rich were more likely to receive treatment. Notice here, however, that Jesus is speaking about the sick in general, regardless of their social or economic status.

The meaning of this proverb seems obvious, but sometimes the simplest teachings can be the most difficult to follow. How would Jesus react to the knowledge that in a wealthy Western country such as the United States, for example, over 40 million people have no health insurance? That in many countries, some people can receive faster and better health care simply because they can pay for it, while others must wait, sometimes for months? That many in the world die of preventable and curable diseases simply because they can't get the medication they need? Although this little saying may seem deceptively simple, it states a clear priority that the sick, regardless of who they are, should receive care. Clearly this is an urgent challenge for our world today.

3

Old Wine Is Good

"And no one puts new wine
into old wineskins …"
Luke 5:37-39

In Luke 5:36, Jesus instructs that it is not wise to sew a piece from a new garment onto an old garment, for the fabric will tear and the new piece will not match the old. In the following three verses he describes the incompatibility of new wine and old wineskins. He says it would be ridiculous to put new wine into old wineskins, for the skins will break, the wine will be lost, and the skins destroyed. Rather, new wine should be poured into new wineskins. Finally, Jesus adds that no one, after drinking old wine, desires new wine, and he closes with the comment that the old is good.

The point of these teachings is straightforward. It is silly to mix two things that are incompatible because the combination will produce destruction and loss. What is more, Luke's gospel values old wine more than the new.

As we saw in the previous chapter, proverbial teachings resonate with wisdom traditions. It was common to compare the old with the new in various Jewish and Greek literary settings. For example, Sirach 9:10 compares old friends to new friends, instructing the reader that new friends are like new wine and not equal to old friends, for the friendship needs to mature. Old friendships must be maintained, presumably because over time friends prove their faithfulness (cf. Sirach 6:14-17).

The gospels of Matthew (19:16-17) and Mark (2:21-22) contain comparable teachings about garments, wine and wineskins, but omit the reference to not drinking new wine after drinking the old. (Interestingly, this does appear in the noncanonical Gospel of Thomas [47:3].)[1] In Matthew and Mark, these teachings appear in the context of Jesus defending his disciples from the criticism that they do not fast like John the Baptist's disciples do. Because there is no mention of the value of the old wine, the teachings in these gospels have often been interpreted as comparing John the Baptist's disciples (the old) and those of Jesus (the new), or between the parent religion of Judaism (the old) and the Christian movement (the new). However, the sayings as they are preserved in the Gospel of Luke (and the Gospel of Thomas) argue against such an interpretation. The core of these teachings is simple: do not mix two things that are incompatible and remember to value that which is old.

Although it is tempting to interpret these references to wine and wineskins as symbols of other things, there is no indication, at least on the lips of Jesus, that such a symbolic reading is necessary. In fact, the understanding of the old wine as somehow representative of Judaism and the new wine as representative of Christianity, a common interpretation in the history of Christianity, has had disastrous results. The emphasis upon Christianity as superseding or replacing Judaism has contributed directly to prejudices and catastrophes that found their most destructive manifestation in the Holocaust. There is no indication from the evidence for Jesus' ministry that he wanted to replace his heritage and faith with a new religion. Although Jesus challenged practices and attitudes of his day, the notion that Judaism had become defunct and obsolete finds no support in his teachings. He does not teach Christian supersessionism (the idea that Christianity has supplanted other forms of religion, especially Judaism).

These points are crucial for Christians to remember. Our world has borne witness to much religious prejudice, oppression and conflict. If Christians take the attitude that somehow their religion is superior to others, they will find it difficult to respect and appreciate the many and diverse religions of the world, and further violence will inevitably ensue. Rather than focusing on which religion is "true," we do well to heed Jesus' wisdom and focus on how to treat other people, regardless of their beliefs.

4

Rules Can Be Broken

"The sabbath was made
for humankind, and not
humankind for the sabbath."
Mark 2:27

The importance of observing the sabbath cannot be overestimated in first-century Palestinian Judaism. This practice of resting on the seventh day finds its roots in biblical traditions such as Genesis 2:3 ("So God blessed the seventh day and hallowed it, because on it God rested") and the fourth commandment as expressed in Exodus 20:8 ("Remember the sabbath day"), and it is associated with such stories as the rescue of the Israelites from slavery in Egypt (Deuteronomy 5:15). At different points in the history of Israel, rules about behaviour on the sabbath were enforced. There is evidence that during a revolt in the second century BCE, Jewish fighters opted for death rather than enter battle on the sabbath (1 Maccabees 2:29-41). As a result, the teaching on the Sabbath changed: above all, life was to be protected, and thus it was acceptable to defend oneself during the day of rest. This idea that the preservation of life was more important than sabbath observance continued to influence sabbath regulations as they developed over time.

The saying in Mark 2:27 appears only in the Gospel of Mark, although the subsequent phrase, "so the Son of Man is lord even of the sabbath," is shared by Matthew and Luke. The gospel writer places the little saying directly after a debate about what is not permitted during the sabbath. As Jesus' disciples were stripping heads of grain on the day of rest they ran into some Pharisees who complained that the disciples should not be doing such things at that time. Plucking heads of grain, like sowing, plowing, hunting, baking, and other forms of work, were not allowed on the sabbath. Jesus responds with a story about David, who gave the bread of the Presence, reserved only for priests, to his hungry companions when there was nothing else to eat. Jesus tops off the story with his statement about the sabbath.

Mark 2:27 has caused many scholars to scratch their heads over its precise meaning. Is the sabbath not important to Jesus? Does he deliberately violate sabbath observance? Other gospel stories describe Jesus healing people and exorcising demons – e.g., the tale of the man with the withered hand (Mark 3:1-6) and the man with the unclean spirit (Mark 1:21-28) – on the sabbath. How can we understand the saying in Mark 2:27 in light of such stories?

Jesus never directly attacks the existence or worth of the sabbath. He does not repudiate Jewish law, even though he challenges aspects of it. What he does do is focus on human well-being. For

Jesus, what seems to be paramount is meeting basic human needs, whether by providing enough food or healing the sick. Prayer, worship and rest are important dimensions of life and of celebrating our relationship to God, but not when they endanger human life. Indeed, many Jews of Jesus' day would likely have agreed with this point, as is evident in the various exceptions to regulations about sabbath observance that appeared both before and after Jesus.

In short, we could interpret this saying this way: rules are important, but when life and well-being are at stake, rules are meant to be broken.

5

Share the Light

"No one after lighting a lamp
puts it under the bushel basket,
but on the lampstand, and it gives
light to all the house."
Matthew 5:15

This proverbial saying appears in multiple contexts throughout the gospels. Here it is embedded in Matthew's famous Sermon on the Mount (Matthew 5-7), a speech directed to the disciples in Matthew. In this particular context the saying emphasizes that the disciples are "the light of the world" (Matthew 5:14) and the "salt of the earth" (Matthew 5:13). As a community the disciples are to shine before others so that others may see their "good works" and give glory to God (Matthew 5:16). Versions of the saying also appear in Mark 4:21 and Luke 8:16, where again they address the disciples, but in these instances function as illustrations of the disciples' ability to understand the parables and their responsibility to interpret the mysterious little stories to others. Luke uses the saying a second time in chapter 11 (Luke 11:33) where he groups it with other teachings about the light that illumines the body (11:36).

The variety of applications of the saying reveals how the gospel writers would take a teaching of Jesus and apply it to different contexts, just as we read and interpret biblical texts in different settings today. Many of Jesus' teachings are quite general and thus can easily serve as illustrations and applications in multiple situations. This does not mean that the teachings can be made to mean whatever one wishes, however, and thus it is necessary to place the saying in its historical context in order to avoid misunderstanding its meaning altogether.

In Judaism, light was a symbol of life, knowledge, peace and blessing whereas darkness was indicative of evil, suffering, chaos and suffering. One recalls that in Genesis, God's first creation is light. Greek philosophers would refer to light as illustrative of divine and spiritual realities. In the prologue to the Gospel of John, we observe the "Word" characterized as the life that "was the light of all people" (John 1:4) shining "in the darkness" (John 1:5). In several ancient apocalyptic communities where it was anticipated that the divine would intervene and save the righteous very soon, light was often associated with the believing community; those outside it were seen as being doomed to constant darkness. Thus the notion that light equals good and darkness equals bad was a common one among numerous groups in antiquity. For ancient people, moreover, darkness was not simply the absence of light. Darkness pushed out light just as light could push out darkness. Thus although we think of darkness as the absence of light, in the first century the two things were understood to be opposing forces.

A first-century Jewish peasant house typically consisted of one room, in the middle of which was placed the lampstand that served to keep the darkness at bay. Often at the end of the day the lamp was put out under a bushel basket in order to avoid having too much smoke settle into the house when people were going to sleep. Thus the notion of putting a lamp under a basket is not strange. It would be ridiculous, however, to light a lamp and then immediately put it under a basket. The purpose of light was to combat the darkness, and thus one should not cover it up. The point of the saying, therefore, seems to be that one should not conceal something that is done to serve a useful and important purpose, for to do so would be to destroy it and snuff it out.

To some extent, this teaching has been used in a negative way throughout the past two thousand years, suggesting that those who have the light, "the enlightened," must shine on those who are in darkness. Such an interpretation is dangerous because it can serve to set up an "us and them" or "insider/outsider" mentality that creates barriers between people. It is better to resist thinking of the light as specific to certain groups or individuals. Instead, we might imagine the light to be particular gifts we can share, to make the world better, or signs of hope flickering in the midst of the suffering and confusion that surround us. There is no point in hiding these gifts or extinguishing these signs of hope; the world needs all the gifts and hope it can get! Nor is Jesus calling for people to boast of their expertise or assume a superior status over others; rather, he is saying that if we have created something or done something useful or enlightening, share it and allow it to serve its purpose.

6

Prophets and Honour

"Prophets are not without honour,
except in their hometown,
and among their own kin,
and in their own house."
Mark 6:4

Two central values for ancient Mediterranean peoples were honour and shame. Honour was something men could inherit by being born into an honourable family or acquire through feats of courage, control of family, and upright reputation within the community. Women were to uphold shame through modesty, obedience, a quiet demeanor and hard work. A man's honour could be challenged, however, in a multitude of ways. If a male head of household's wife, daughter, sister or niece flouted his orders or became involved in a scandal, the event would reflect upon him, and he could lose honour in the eyes of the community. He would be perceived as weak for not being able to control the women in his family. (Imagine the plight of Mary's father at the news of her being pregnant before she is married.) If a man's son behaved recklessly or wasted money, this behaviour would reflect negatively on the father. Such an observation adds a new dimension to the parable of the Prodigal Son (Luke 11:15-32); the behaviour of the father in the story is contrary to what would be expected of a first-century Palestinian Jew who had been disgraced by his offspring.

Another relevant contextual issue is the notion of a dyadic personality. (The term "dyadism" comes from a Greek word for a "pair"; the dyadic personality is someone who needs another in order to know who she or he is.) People in the ancient world did not perceive themselves primarily as individuals, as we tend to do in modern Western cultures. Rather, they understood themselves in relation to the larger community, including the extended family, the village, the city or the nation. How other people perceived someone defined how that person understood himself or herself, regardless of social rank.

These features of first-century Mediterranean life are important to recall when approaching literature from the period. In Mark 6:4 we find an unusual and memorable saying that is well attested in the gospel tradition, appearing in Matthew, Mark, Luke, John and the Gospel of Thomas. In Mark's (and Matthew's and Luke's) context, Jesus arrives in his hometown, Nazareth, and begins to teach in the synagogue. Those who hear him teaching are surprised. They ask where he obtained such wisdom and deeds of power, for "is not this the carpenter, the son of Mary and brother of James and Joses and Judas and Simon, and are not his sisters here with us?" (Mark 6:3). Right here one notices that Jesus is understood in terms of his family; his reputation is based, in part, on his relationships to others. The villagers cannot understand how a mere carpenter, whose relations they know, can possess such wisdom and power. Jesus does not come from an honourable family (manual labourers were not highly regarded). Although the villagers are at first impressed by his actions, it does not make sense to them that he should be doing such things. Not surprisingly, they take offense at him (Mark 6:3) because he is violating the codes of honour and shame. He is stepping out of place and behaving in a manner that is inappropriate to his family status and station in life.

Jesus does not make any apologies for his actions but responds that prophets are not without honour except in their hometown. This is a daring thing to say – he is insulting the villagers by stating that it is only among his own village and kin that his honour is not recognized, thereby implying that outsiders do recognize his honour. This is a serious blow to those who think they know Jesus, for in antiquity, people were automatically suspicious of outsiders and classified them as enemies until proven otherwise. As a result, Mark's gospel states that "he could do no deed of power there, except that he laid his hands upon a few sick people and cured them. And he was amazed at their unbelief" (Mark 6:5-6). Faith, a key theme in Mark's gospel, is required in order for Jesus to perform mighty deeds, but faith is something that the villagers lack.

A variety of issues arise from this teaching. Particularly interesting is Jesus' feisty willingness to challenge the pervasive and often oppressive system of honour and shame. This system set the standard for acceptable behaviour; to challenge it could lead to rejection by family and village which would, in turn, have a serious impact on one's ability to survive in a largely agrarian, kinship-based society. Jesus' response to the townspeople's offense at him was thus a dangerous one, for he risked their total rejection of him (which is indeed the outcome in Luke's version of the story).

Given the huge cultural divide between the society of contemporary North America and that of the first-century Mediterranean region, it is often difficult to determine how Jesus' teachings are relevant. As I mentioned in the first chapter, many of his teachings were radical for his day: this is certainly true of Mark 6. Although honour and shame do not play a central role in North America today, we have our own codes that dictate social standing. For example, we stereotype certain people and groups, or limit possibilities for people based on their background. Some unhealthy practices and systems have become so normative in our culture, we do not even question them. Jesus took considerable risk in responding to his neighbours the way he did. What are we willing to risk in order to challenge those values and systems that do not contribute to the flourishing of all creatures that inhabit our world, and are gradually destroying the planet itself?

7

Crossing Boundaries

"It is not what goes into the mouth
that defiles a person, but it is what
comes out of the mouth that defiles."
Matthew 15:11

Most, if not all, human societies have explicit or implicit notions of what constitutes "pure" versus "impure." Many anthropologists have observed that establishing boundaries between what is considered clean and unclean – whether this pertains to places, persons, things, or actions – defines a system of meaning that in turn helps the members of the society to make sense of life. When we cross that boundary and move from pure to impure, we must go through a process of purification.

Lines between pure and impure, clean and unclean, were clearly drawn in first-century Judaism. Many of the codes determining ritual impurity are set forth in the Book of Leviticus (e.g., Leviticus 11–21); they are also articulated and further developed in the Palestinian and Babylonian Talmuds, or collections of rabbinic teachings, gathered between 200 and 500 CE. Certainly, purity codes were important in Jesus' day and, according to the gospels, led to controversy and debate between Jesus and other Jews.

Matthew 15:1-20 is an example of an argument that arises between Jesus and some Pharisees and scribes who come to him from Jerusalem. They ask Jesus why his disciples do not wash their hands before they eat, as ritual washing before consuming food was an important religious practice. Jesus responds by accusing the Pharisees of breaking the Lord's commandments to honour father and mother, and to not speak evil of one's parents, in order to uphold their own tradition (and effectively avoid supporting the parents). He calls them hypocrites who honour God with their lips but follow human tradition instead of holy commandments. He then calls the crowd to him and makes the statement about what goes in and what comes out of the mouth, then continues to lambaste the Pharisees, calling them blind guides of the blind. He further elaborates, in Matthew 15:17, that whatever enters the mouth simply enters the stomach and exits into the sewer. What comes out of the mouth, however comes from the heart. It is this that defiles, for it can contain evil intentions, murder, adultery, and so on. In conclusion, Jesus repeats that what leaves the mouth can render a person unclean, "but to eat with unwashed hands does not defile" (Matthew 15:20).

In this discussion, Jesus has squarely challenged the purity codes of his day. He has transgressed the boundaries by insisting that certain ritual practices, such as what one eats, or whether one washes one's hands before a meal, are not important. Rather, the gospel emphasizes that things coming out of the mouth, such as evil intentions, lead to immoral actions. Matthew stresses Jesus' conflict with the Pharisees. His is the only gospel in which they are accused of being blind guides at this moment, and later on in the gospel (chapter 23) they are especially vilified. The author of the gospel, probably writing around 80–90 CE, may have been living in a context in which there was considerable debate about what it meant to be Jewish, and in which the Pharisees, not especially prominent in Jesus' day, had emerged as a significant group within Judaism. For Matthew, a true Jew was one who accepted Jesus as the Messiah, and so Matthew attacks other groups within Judaism, such as Pharisees. The saying in question becomes, for Matthew, another way of demonstrating that Jesus, the Messiah, was counter to the ways of the Pharisees.

If we take the saying out of its context in Matthew, remove the moralizing interpretation of Matthew 15:18, and simply imagine it as a short saying on its own, we might interpret it differently. Mark's version, which is generally thought to be more original than Matthew's, simply states that "there is nothing outside a person that by going in can defile, but the things that come out are what defile" (Mark 7:15). Notice the lack of reference to a mouth here. The teaching is quite general; it need not refer specifically to food nor to immoral behaviour caused by speech. One might even read it as a witty statement, if Jesus is referring to concrete things that enter and exit the body through the natural orifices, for indeed those things that exit the body through the physical channels would be defiling. However, Jesus is not specific, and thus this broad statement serves as a sweeping rejection of the established tradition of boundaries between clean and unclean. Moreover, it is precisely this generality that draws people in, for it causes them to wonder and think about what Jesus is up to here. As mentioned in Chapter 1, Jesus often challenges his listeners to think for themselves; this general, riddle-like saying is evidence of that practice.

In contemporary life, boundaries between pure and impure continue to exist. I do not want to suggest that these boundaries should be destroyed or that they are not important. However, knowing that they are constructions by society may enable us to better critique and evaluate which boundaries are necessary and which are not. Indeed, lines between clean and unclean are often developed precisely to keep the "unclean" on the outside. This sort of boundary setting is cruel and only serves the interests of those with more power. Jesus calls us to challenge this kind of exclusive behaviour.

8

A Kingdom for Children

"Let the little children come
to me, and do not stop them;
for it is to such as these that
the kingdom of God belongs."
Mark 10:14

Life for children in first-century Palestine was
not easy. Their very survival was precarious. The
infant death rate could be as high as 30 per cent,
and many more died before the age of six. Some
estimate that up to 60 per cent of children did not
live to be sixteen. Causes of death included disease, famine, wars and exposure. Orphans were
dependent on handouts, increasing the risk of
starvation or illness. Although Jews did not, many
ancient peoples practised infanticide if there were
too many children, or if they simply did not want
a child.

Socially, children were at the bottom of the
heap in most ancient cultures, including those of
the Mediterranean. Respect was accorded to older
people, and children were expected to obey their

elders. Discipline was often maintained through punishment, including beatings that were sometimes severe. Moreover, sons were valued more than daughters. This gender division reflected the patriarchal attitude found in many societies of the ancient world. Males were understood to be superior to females, as men upheld the honour of the family and village and represented the family to the outside world. As we saw in Chapter 6, females generally focused upon domestic activities to avoid dishonouring their family, and were dependent on the protection of the males.

Despite children's lack of status and power, and the differences in attitudes towards male versus female children, the birth of a child was considered a blessing and a gift from God in Judaism. A woman's chief task in life was to bear children; we can understand the gratitude of Elizabeth in Luke's gospel story when she discovers she is pregnant. Throughout the Bible, God is often portrayed as being at work through children. One of the most striking examples is that of Jesus himself. Despite his seemingly humble origins, he is given a name that means "the Lord saves," and in Matthew's story of his birth, is visited by three wise men from the East. This is surely an unusual story, for children of Galilean Jews were not normally honoured by wise men from other countries who not only paid homage but brought gifts of gold, frankincense and myrrh.

Mark's gospel highlights the notion that children have a significant role to play. This particular teaching is set within the context of people, probably mothers, bringing children to Jesus so that he might touch them. No doubt the mothers are aware of the vulnerabilities of their babies. They seek Jesus' touch because it may protect the children from threatening forces, such as the evil eye, a notion that one could be cursed by a malevolent look from a stranger or enemy. In this scene, Jesus' disciples try to prevent the parents from bringing the children to Jesus, who becomes indignant, saying, "Let the little children come to me." He goes on to say that the kingdom belongs to these children. Thus we observe a striking reversal. The children, so often viewed as insignificant in the ancient world, are accorded great status.

Throughout Mark's gospel, children become models for discipleship. The disciples, in contrast, are often fearful, lack faith in Jesus, and even abandon him at his arrest. For example, in Mark 9:33-37, the disciples admit to Jesus that they had been arguing about who among them was the greatest. Jesus responds that whoever wants to be first must be last. Then he takes a little child into his arms, saying, "Whoever welcomes one such child in my name, welcomes me." This juxtaposition of the disciples, who are arguing about power and who will be "first," and a helpless child, no doubt considered to be "the last," suggests that the child is the better model of discipleship. Moreover, when the disciples are arguing over who will succeed Jesus after his death, Jesus picks up the little child, an action that some suggest could be compared to an adoption ritual. In other words, the one who will succeed Jesus is not to be found among the disciples, but among the most vulnerable in society.

The need to love and care for children, which we take for granted today, is upheld in the example of Jesus. But the social significance of statements such as Mark 10:14 can be lost if we remain unaware of the low status of children in Jesus' time. As some scholars have said, children were viewed as "nobodies" in the ancient world, yet Jesus says that the kingdom belongs to them.[2] Who then are the "nobodies" today?

9

The Kingdom and Wealth

"How hard it is for those
who have wealth to enter
the kingdom of God."
Luke 18:24

In the ancient world, all things – honour, power, friendship, land, money, trade goods, water, and
food – were deemed to be of limited supply. Thus,
if a man lost honour, it meant another man (probably his challenger, or someone who had insulted
him) increased his. If one landowner lost land,
another gained. If one person lost money, another
person accumulated more. But unlike modern
capitalist societies, those of the Mediterranean pre-
industrial period did not view those who acquired
wealth in a positive light. The goal in life, for an
ancient person, was to preserve what he or she
had. An individual or family that increased their
land or wealth would be viewed as greedy, for the
prosperous ones were now depriving someone
else of their goods and upsetting the balance and
distribution of wealth within the community. As

the early Christian theologian St. Jerome wrote, "Every rich person is either unjust or the heir of an unjust person."[3]

We don't hear the word "usury" much anymore, but this practice of making money on the use of money was condemned in Jesus' world. People who practised it, such as tax collectors (who in Palestine would pay out a certain amount of their collection to the Romans and keep the rest), merchants (who would buy goods at cost but sell them for more and pocket the profit), and money lenders (who lent money at interest), were regarded as exploitative and greedy. Numerous texts throughout the Second Testament, notably the Letter of James (e.g., James 5:1-6), condemn people who act in such a manner.

These attitudes have important implications for the interpretation of this teaching. In all three synoptic gospels, the saying appears after Jesus has been approached by a rich man (a "ruler," in Luke's gospel) who asks Jesus what he must do to inherit eternal life. Jesus tells him to obey the commandments. The man indicates that he does; Jesus then informs him that he must sell all he owns, distribute the money among the poor, and follow Jesus. The man looks at him sadly, "for he was very rich," and Jesus states how hard it is for the rich to enter the kingdom. Jesus then elaborates, using hyperbole, that it is easier for the biggest animal in Palestine, the camel, to go through the smallest opening, the eye of a needle, than for the rich to enter the kingdom, or domain, of God.

What do we make of these teachings today, living in a society in which usury is central to our economic system and there is such an emphasis upon making money? Some experts talk about the "growth in the economy" as if everyone will get more. But is this really true? Might we do well to take advice from the ancients that all things are in limited supply? Certainly those working to preserve the environment are well aware that natural resources, such as water, exist in finite quantities, and that when one group gets more, another usually loses out. What would happen if we looked at other commodities in such a way, so that when one individual or group makes a big gain we investigate who were the losers, and how much they lost?

Furthermore, instead of focusing so much on increasing wealth, we could ask, "What does a person need to live in dignity?" Most people would agree that basic levels of food, water, clothing, shelter, health care, education, and the opportunity to contribute in some way to the larger community are essential for a life of dignity. The level of these needs must be determined in a broad context: in light of the needs of people not only in our local communities, but around the world. In other words, do we need to use water to keep our lawns green all summer or our cars sparkling clean, when people in other parts of the world lack access to clean water? Our ever-increasing consumption of oil is another good example. Why do we expect unlimited access to oil when other countries have scarcely any? How can we start to decrease our dependence on oil to restore the balance? When we think creatively about these issues, we can rethink, collectively, our economic systems and how they often exploit certain people, especially those at the bottom of the ladder.

These are hard teachings in a world that is so focused on wealth, and a world in which those who make obscene amounts of money are often grudgingly admired. Given the discomfort that these teachings cause many today, one can understand why Jesus' words would have been disturbing to those who had wealth in his own day. Perhaps these teachings are even more difficult today than they were in Jesus' day, for the pursuit of more, as opposed to the maintenance of what one already possesses, seems to be pervasive. If we can resist the temptation to fall prey to our consumer culture, perhaps we can edge a little closer to this notion of kingdom of which Jesus often spoke. After all, Jesus' message is clear: "You cannot serve God and wealth" (Luke 16:13).

10

Born from Above

"No one can see the
kingdom of God without
being born from above"
John 3:3

This particular teaching is unique to the Gospel of John, although the notion of being reborn or being like children in order to enter the kingdom, as we have seen elsewhere, appears throughout the gospels. However, the context for the saying, a discussion between Jesus and the Pharisee Nicodemus, is found only in this gospel.

Nicodemus is identified not only as a Pharisee, but as a member of the Jewish Sanhedrin, a governing body of the Jews. Obviously, he is a person of importance. It is not clear why he comes to see Jesus at night; perhaps he was afraid that others would see him speaking with Jesus, or it may reflect the practice of staying up very late to study Torah. Whatever the reason, notions of darkness and night are symbolic of ignorance and evil in this gospel, and thus this detail underscores Nicodemus' lack of clear understanding as to who is this "teacher who has come from God" (John 3:2).

Nicodemus believes that Jesus is a teacher approved by God because of the signs, or miracles, that Jesus has performed. Earlier in the gospel, Jesus does not trust those who believe in his name because of his signs (John 2:23-25); we see evidence of this distrust in his cool reception of Nicodemus. As many have observed, Nicodemus approaches Jesus with good intentions, but an inadequate understanding of who Jesus really is. As Jesus explains in the ensuing dialogue, he is not only approved by God, he was sent by God "so that the world might be saved through him" (John 3:17).

Jesus' indirect response suggests that Nicodemus' opening statement belies a desire to see the "kingdom of God" – a phrase that appears only in these two verses in this gospel. Jesus states that one must be born "from above" (the Greek word can mean "from above" or "again") in order to see the kingdom. Here, the notion of "seeing" does not mean the ability to view an object visually. It refers to "experiencing" something, as in "see life" (John 3:36). Nicodemus takes Jesus' statement literally and thus asks how a person can be born "again" after having grown old. This misunderstanding, a typical feature of John's gospel, allows Jesus to further elucidate his point. He goes on to say that one must be born of water and the spirit. Clearly Jesus is stressing that he is speaking not of physical birth, but of birth from above, from

God. Nicodemus still cannot understand ("How can these things be?" [John 3:9]). Jesus, after rebuking him, continues to explain the revelation with which God has entrusted him.

This teaching raises significant issues for us today, pointing to some central questions about the nature of faith. Nicodemus, it seems, bases his faith in Jesus upon Jesus' performance of signs. Clearly, for Jesus, this is not enough. Faith, we can infer from the story, is not something that is built upon observable facts, but comes from trusting in the revelation of Jesus, and living out of that trust.

The specific teachings – "No one can see the kingdom of God without being born from above" and "No one can enter the kingdom of God without being born of the water and spirit"(John 3:5) – are impossible to interpret completely, for part of the power of such statements lies in their poetic qualities. However, it is clear that they both point to a new way of seeing. Empowered by the gift of the spirit, people can see and enter "the kingdom of God." Nicodemus cannot seem to get past a literal interpretation of what Jesus is telling him, yet the gospel writer insists that we must go beyond the security of the literal to symbol and metaphor, where meaning is much more difficult to determine. Many of us can relate to Nicodemus' confusion, and think of our own struggles to be open to a new, more imaginative way of seeing the world, instead of constructing meaning based only on quantifiable fact or observation. Yet perhaps we can also remember moments when we have been particularly struck by a feeling or insight that may be hard to put into words, but has led us to seek greater understanding. It is this openness to a new way of seeing that this teaching, and indeed the gospel as a whole, calls us to embrace.

11

Stone Throwing

"Let any among you who
is without sin be the first to
throw a stone at her."
John 8:7

Many of us have probably heard this famous
teaching more than once, possibly in the context of
a reprimand for criticizing other people. This statement is unique to the Gospel of John, as is the story
of the woman caught in adultery, in which it is embedded. What is more, in the various copies of the
Gospel of John that still exist (to our knowledge, no
original copy of any book of the Bible exists), the
story appears in different places, sometimes here in
chapter 8, and sometimes at the end of the gospel.
Several manuscripts of the Gospel of Luke place it
in that gospel! This "roving" aspect of the story indicates that it circulated independently in the early
church before being picked up and integrated into
the gospels at different points in history.

As is well known, the scene is the Mount of
Olives. While Jesus is teaching, some Pharisees and

scribes bring before him a woman who has been caught in adultery. After humiliating the woman by making her stand in front of everyone, they try to trap Jesus, stating that the Law of Moses decrees that such women should be stoned to death and then demanding that Jesus respond. Jesus bends over, drawing on the ground with his finger, and utters the famous words about casting the first stone. He returns to drawing on the ground. Slowly, the audience drifts away, leaving Jesus alone with the woman. He asks her if anyone has condemned her, and she replies that they have not. He then says he does not condemn her either and tells her to go on her way, but to sin no more.

The woman's identity remains a mystery. In the history of the church she has often been identified as Mary Magdalene, but there is no evidence for this opinion. In the story we find out very little about her. Other than Jesus' instruction to her to sin no more, we do not know as to whether she wanted to engage in an adulterous affair. We do not meet her husband or the man with whom she has had the affair. The focus of blame is clearly upon her.

We examined the roles of honour and shame in first-century Mediterranean culture in Chapter 6; this woman is presented as having violated those values. It is not always clear how often the punishment, stoning, was carried out against adulterers in the ancient world, but technically this was the legal punishment. Leviticus 20:10 orders the death penalty for adultery, while Deuteronomy 22:21 indicates that if a woman is found not to be a virgin before marriage, she shall be stoned to death.

Ezekiel 16:38-40 offers further indications that the regular punishment was stoning.

As mentioned in the story, the Pharisees and scribes are trying to trap Jesus. If he says that the woman should go free, then he will clearly be defying the Law of Moses, but if he agrees to have her stoned, he may be in trouble with the Roman authorities. In the Gospel of John, the Sanhedrin, of which Nicodemus was a member, did not have the legal power to execute people within the Roman empire; there is some information that around the year 30 CE, the Romans took away the Jewish authorities' right to put people to death. The Pharisees and scribes want to catch Jesus so he can be punished.

Jesus does not allow himself to be caught, however. Rather than making a decision about her fate, he asks the woman's accusers to examine themselves. One can easily imagine the downcast faces of those who have brought the woman to Jesus as they realize that they are not without sin, and perhaps feel their shamelessness that they have been so quick to seek the death of this defenseless woman who stands terrified before them. Jesus has effectively defused the situation. The focus is no longer on the woman's behaviour, nor upon trapping Jesus, but on each person examining himself or herself.

This teaching is a timeless one. We are often quick to blame others for their mistakes without considering our own. To face honestly and take responsibility for the hurtful things we say and do is difficult, but in this teaching, Jesus demands it.

Indeed, he has compassion on the woman, he does not condemn her, but he tells her to sin no more, indicating that she must take responsibility for her actions. The teaching is relevant not only for individuals, but for groups, societies and nations. It is easy to blame other people, or other countries, but what about us? We must continue to accept the challenge to look ourselves in the mirror with a critical eye, and to take responsibility for our actions before blaming or criticizing others.

12

The Poor Are Blessed

"Blessed are you who are poor."
Luke 6:20

We saw in Chapter 9 that the wealthy in Jesus' day were also understood to be the greedy because they were taking more than they needed and causing others to lose out. "To be labeled 'rich' was therefore a social and moral statement as much as an economic one,"[4] according to biblical scholars Bruce Malina and Richard Rohrbaugh. Likewise, the "poor" in the ancient world were not only those who had little, but those who had lost part or all of what they once had. In addition, poverty referred not only to economic deficiency, but to a loss of honour, power, and often health. In the Second Testament, poor people are often associated with those who are humiliated (James 2:1-7), or who are sick, naked and blind (Revelation 3:17). In general, poor people were weak in every sense of the word. For this reason, some scholars have argued that the conflict between the strong and the weak that the apostle Paul must contend with in the Corinthian community is precisely a conflict between rich and poor Christians (1 Corinthians 1:26-31).

By proclaiming that the poor are "blessed," Jesus is saying that the poor are now honourable. Some have translated "blessed" (the Greek word is *makarios*) as "happy" or "congratulations." However you translate it, Jesus is turning the honour and shame codes upside down once again by stating that those who are seen as dishonourable and humiliated are the honourable ones. He goes on to say that the kingdom of God belongs to these poor, to these beggars and destitute people. Some have commented that for Jesus, the kingdom of God belongs to "nobodies," as mentioned in Chapter 8.[5] This theme is continued in the remaining beatitudes, or blessings, when Jesus congratulates those who are hungry and those who mourn or weep. He assures the hungry that they will be filled and the sad that they will laugh. He is proclaiming the kingdom for them and offering them hope that their misery will indeed end, not in some distant future, but in the here and now.

One can appreciate, from these teachings, why the marginalized in Jesus' day would be attracted to his words. At the same time, those who had power and wealth would be profoundly disturbed by such teachings. Who is Jesus to declare that God's kingdom, God's empire and realm, belongs to poor, sick people? In a culture of limited goods, this teaching would be threatening to the rich, for it implies that the social order is different in God's domain. If the hungry are to be fed, then the full might not receive as much as they have come to expect. Indeed, by declaring that the poor are now honourable, Jesus is upsetting the entire social order and redefining how people are to perceive and behave towards one another. Thus we see that not only does Jesus offer hope to many, but he poses a threat to the elite.

Some of the Hebrew prophets, such as Isaiah (Isaiah 61), also cried out on behalf of the poor, and care for the destitute continued within the early church after Jesus' death. Paul upheld these teachings by collecting money for the poor of Jerusalem (Galatians 2:10) and insisting that "God chose what is low and despised in the world, things that are not, to reduce to nothing things that are, so that no one might boast in the presence of God" (1 Corinthians 1:28-29). This is a hard message to accept. Paul's subsequent rocky relationship with the Corinthians indicates that they did not take kindly to his words.

Few would argue that this teaching is any easier to hear today. We have witnessed this type of radical wisdom in the lives of such well-known figures as of St. Francis of Assisi, Blessed Mother Teresa or Dorothy Day, the co-founder of the Catholic Worker movement. Countless unknown people who live simply, sharing all that they have with those in need, continue this modelling of Gospel living. Although such individuals and groups remain the minority, they stand out as examples for all of us to reflect upon as we attempt to live out our commitments.

Yet it is important to focus not only on the individual or small community lifestyle that such examples embody, but on the social and political dimensions of Jesus' words. To say that the poor are blessed means, surely, that the poor deserve all the good things that anyone else receives. The question of what a person needs in order to live a life of dignity, asked in Chapter 9, is relevant here. If we want to embody, socially, this particular saying, we need to re-examine our social structures. If everyone has enough, we will no longer need food banks, homeless shelters, and so on. Perhaps this dream of universal well-being is unrealistic, but Jesus still encourages us to share more fairly, which means that some will have to give up portions of their wealth. Such a call directly challenges the economic and social systems of the majority of the world's nations at this time. But there are ways to improve these systems. Maybe we cannot not all live as St. Francis or Dorothy Day did, but we can, at the very least, "live simply so that others may simply live," as the bumper sticker says, and work for legislation and policies that will support a more equitable distribution of goods.

13

Turn the Other Cheek

"If anyone strikes you on the
cheek, offer the other also."
Luke 6:29

Violence surrounds us. Whether it is in the
newspapers, on television, or in our neighbour-
hood, we cannot escape it. The power of this violence over us as individuals and communities is
overwhelming. Not only can it cause trauma and
fear, it promotes aggressive behaviour in us, for we
often learn how to act by imitating other people. If
we see others acting in a cruel or aggressive manner, we may start doing the same. To counteract
such violence, then, we need models of peaceful
conduct.

Jesus' teaching in both Matthew's Sermon on
the Mount and Luke's Sermon on the Plain provides one such model. Violence permeated the
ancient landscape just as much as it does today.
Rape, beatings, war and random violence were
pervasive. In Luke's version of this teaching, Jesus
states that we should love our enemies, do good to

those who hate us, bless those who curse us, and pray for those who abuse us. If someone strikes us on the cheek, we are to turn the other also (Luke 6:27-29).

Such an instruction is counter to the expected response of someone who is abused, violated or hit: if a man wants to uphold his honour after being attacked, he should hit back; he should not put up with such treatment. Yet Jesus is not advocating passive acceptance of abuse. With the "turn the other cheek" example, he has created a type of parody, or an exaggerated example that even has a humorous effect. No one would ever dream of letting someone hit them again after being slapped on the cheek. Such a reaction is laughable. By offering his listeners such a shocking, even silly, instruction, Jesus would make people stop in their tracks and reconsider standard modes of behaviour. Jesus forces people to think by offering extreme, but not impossible, examples. This does not mean becoming a passive victim, allowing others to walk all over us. By turning the other cheek, the "victim" indicates that he or she is not willing to play the honour/shame game, and breaks the cycle of violence. It is a creative, self-respecting response that might cause the aggressor to skulk away in confusion, or perhaps seek reconciliation.

A modern example of this response to violence can be found in a true story preserved by Muriel Lester, a longtime member of the International Fellowship of Reconciliation. Lester narrates the plight of a Viennese family at the end of World War II, when Russian troops marched triumphantly into Vienna. The family knew that there was a good chance the troops would plunder their home and perhaps rape their beautiful daughter, as is often the case in the aftermath of one army defeating another. When the troops banged on the door, the family did not try to keep them out, but welcomed them in, offering them coffee and hospitality. Soon the mother was playing folk songs on the piano, which the troops joined in singing, finding similarities to their own songs. The soldiers inquired about the family's son, whose picture stood on the piano, to which the family replied, "He was killed in the war ... in Russia." The troops realized that it was time to go back to their barracks and, thanking the family, asked if they could return. The family replied, "Please do. And bring your friends."[6]

This Viennese family had clearly done the unexpected, for rather than reacting with fear and aggression, they bravely welcomed in the soldiers. The family knew that the troops were simply young men, most of whom had been conscripted into the army and would have preferred to be at home. By warmly welcoming in the soldiers and focusing on what they had in common, the family effectively dissolved any aggression the soldiers may have felt. What could have been a violent situation resulted in a peaceful and perhaps even joyful encounter.

We need more models of peaceful behaviour in our violence-ridden world. We have the great examples of Gandhi, Martin Luther King Jr., Leo Tolstoy, and contemporary figures such as American three-time Nobel Peace Prize nominee

Kathy Kelly and the Buddhist monk Thich Nhat Hanh, all of whom have provided creative responses to violence and injustice that do not simply give in, but seek non-violently to achieve reconciliation and well-being for those who are suffering. It is important to know their stories, but also to seek out methods of easing aggression, such as non-violence training workshops, which we can incorporate into our everyday lives. Other forms of daily practice, such as prayer and meditation, can help us confront the violence and anger we feel within ourselves as we face the stresses and frustrations of a complex and often impersonal world. Through such disciplined practice, done individually and in community, we can become models for others and, slowly but surely, spread the desire for peaceful resolution. Spreading this desire will not be easy, nor will it avoid suffering and pain, but it is the method that Jesus practised. He offered an imaginative response to a typical situation, a response which, because of its novelty, caused people to pause and reconsider. As the poet W.H. Auden once wrote, "Prohibit sharply the rehearsed response."[7]

14

Give to Those in Need

"Give to everyone
who begs from you."
Luke 6:30

In the ancient Mediterranean, a small elite held
the majority of wealth and power; the next level
consisted of merchants, traders and military; and
then there were the masses of poor, who laboured
day by day, often on land they did not own. Many
people, such as orphans, widows, and sick people,
practically slid off the social scale and survived
primarily through begging.

Yet, interestingly, some people idealized begging, at least in theory. We see this attitude in some
of the letters and texts about the Cynics, a group of
counter-cultural wanderers who lampooned social
convention and preached internal freedom and
self-sufficiency. The Cynics taught that one should
be free of possessions, and thus in some texts they
advocate begging. For example, Pseudo-Diogenes
writes to Crates, "Ask for bread even from the
statues in the market place as you enter it. In a way,

such a practice is good, for you will meet men more unfeeling than statues."[8] Not surprisingly, some of Jesus' teachings, such as the statement that the Son of Man has nowhere to lay his head (Luke 9:58), which suggests that Jesus was homeless, are comparable to Cynic teachings. Moreover, given the Hellenization of Palestine, Jesus could have come into contact with Cynic philosophers. He may have had many things in common with them.

If we also consider that Jesus said such things as "blessed are the poor," and strongly criticized hoarding wealth, the statement about giving to all who beg from you is not unexpected. What makes it an unusual teaching for the ancient world is the fact that it stresses giving to everyone, not to specific people. Reciprocal relations in antiquity could be divided into three categories: a) generalized reciprocity, practised within kinship groups, in which people gave according to need and often did not expect a return; b) balanced reciprocity, wherein a return of equal amounts was expected, characteristic of neighbourly relations; and c) negative reciprocity, in which one side seeks a gain without having to provide a return, typical of relations to strangers. Thus, what makes Jesus' teaching distinctive is that he is advocating generalized reciprocity, but not to specific family members. He exhorts generosity to everyone who begs, which could include family, neighbours *and* strangers.

If someone is begging, either because she or he has met with misfortune or has chosen such a lifestyle, as the Cynics or Jesus and his followers did, then that person depends upon the benevolence of others to meet her or his needs. Advocating generosity towards such people preserves the moral teaching of Jesus, already encountered in this book, that all should be able to live with their basic needs met not because they get what they deserve, but because they are human beings. Again, Jesus is not the first to proclaim this teaching. It reaches back into the teachings of the First Testament, such as those found in the Book of Isaiah, which cries out, "Seek justice, rescue the oppressed, defend the orphan, and plead for the widow" (Isaiah 1:17), or Zechariah, which says, "Show kindness and mercy to one another; do not oppress the widow, the orphan, the alien, or the poor" (Zechariah 7:9-10).

Caring for those who have little or nothing imitates the actions of God, who throughout the stories of the First Testament comes to the aid of the oppressed and the needy. This vision of God is preserved in the Second Testament, when Jesus says to his followers, "Ask, and it will be given to you" (Luke 11:9-13), or when the Letter of James tells those seeking wisdom to "ask God, who gives to all generously and ungrudgingly" (James 1:5). Jesus wants us to model our behaviour on the actions of God, who provides for all. The biblical image of God reveals one who does not offer special favours to the wealthy or to those of high status; rather, God is often portrayed as showing special concern for the poor, regardless of how they came to live in poverty.

Precisely because of the modern emphasis on wealth and success, these are very difficult teachings to accept for many today. In fact, many people resent it when someone in need asks them for money, and most of us can think of a time when we simply ignored the person on the street who was begging. Sometimes we feel despair as well, for offering a few quarters to a beggar does not seem to make any difference. But it probably makes a difference to the person begging. What is more, there are many other things we can do, from working in homeless shelters to lobbying our elected leaders for better programs and services so that fewer people will need to live on the street. Jesus often spoke in metaphors, but here, we do well to take his teaching literally.

15

The Lord's Prayer

"Father, hallowed be your name."
Luke 11:2

This line is the beginning of the Lord's Prayer, or Our Father. Found in Matthew and Luke, it is thought to go back to *Quelle*, the sayings source known as "Q." The prayer is different in each of these gospels. It is longer in Matthew's gospel, for example, including references to God's will being done and the request to "rescue us from the evil one" (Matthew 6:13). It is hard to know exactly how much of the series of petitions goes back to the historical Jesus, as the gospel writers have edited their sources to suit the overall themes and contexts of their gospels. I will thus engage each form of the prayer to some extent, with a focus on what scholars deem to be the series of petitions that authentically come from Jesus.

The statement "hallowed be your name" refers to the notion of God being distinctive and set apart from other things. Another way of putting this idea is "let your name be holy." Matthew refers to

"Our Father in heaven," while Luke simply says, "Father." Luke's version is thought to be earlier, as Matthew has a penchant for adding "heaven" (the Greek is literally "in the heavens") to his sources throughout his gospel.

Next appears the simple request "Your kingdom come." Matthew has an adjoining line, "Your will be done, on earth as in heaven." Again, this is generally understood to be a Matthean addition. The word "kingdom," however, requires some comment here. Because modern Western people do not usually think of political entities as "kingdoms," the translation "kingdom" can be misleading. The Greek word used in the gospels is *basileia*, which can be an explicitly political term; thus, some modern translations use words and phrases such as "dominion," "empire" or "imperial rule," as these provide a clearer political connotation. In other words, the request asks that God's imperial realm be made manifest on earth. Considering that Jesus and his followers were living within a Roman empire, talk of another empire would likely have been disturbing to those who represented and upheld the power of the state. Although today people may not automatically think of this prayer in political terms, in the ancient world the deliberate contrast between God's realm and Caesar's realm would have been obvious.

The next petition asks for bread for the day. Such a request would be highly relevant to a first-century Palestinian peasant, for whom bread was a main staple, and who would not think about bread for the long term but simply hope to have enough for each day. The prayer is thus calling for one's basic needs to be met. It is focused not upon theories or ideas, but upon providing food for an empty stomach.

The next line differs from one gospel to the other. Luke asks for forgiveness of sin, while Matthew asks for forgiveness of debts. Many scholars think that Matthew's reference to debts – that is, financial and material debts – is the older version, although Luke may have simply understood "sins" to be a reasonable synonym for debts. Again, the notion of providing for material circumstances is in evidence here. The petition asks for relief from debts, a concrete and meaningful request that, if granted, would have brought great relief to poor people in Palestine. Moreover, it indicates that those making the request are willing to forgive the debts of those indebted to them.

The concluding line, "do not bring us to the time of trial," is also a practical request. It asks that people not be subjected to one trial after another. We could say that it asks for a reprieve from hardship for a suffering group of people. It also reveals that people who pray this prayer place complete trust in God to provide such relief. Matthew's final line, "rescue us from the evil one," is a Matthean addition.

In sum, these lines provide a picture of what Jesus and the preservers of his teachings imagined God's kingdom to be. It was a kingdom or empire in which all had bread or sustenance for the day, where people were not indebted to one another, and where trials and sufferings were alleviated.

Moreover, there is nothing to indicate that this rule of God is solely in the future, in some sort of heavenly afterlife. Rather, Jesus wants God's rule to be imposed here and now. It is this call for a radically different world order that no doubt disturbed some of those higher ups who came into contact with these teachings, for it would have threatened their social status and power. Once again, we see how Jesus' teachings are counter-cultural and subversive to his society.

Many Christians pray the Lord's Prayer every day, or at least every time they go to church. Certainly, some think of the social and political implications of the prayer, but because it is prayed so often, it is easy to recite it mechanically, without reflecting on what we are asking. If we consider how poor people from ancient times would have heard these requests, we might rethink the implications of such a prayer for our time. Imagine a planet in which everyone had enough to eat for the day! Consider a world where people and countries were not indebted to other people and institutions! Although such a world is hard to fathom, these characteristics are typical of Jesus' vision of the kingdom. Moreover, although the prayer asks for God to impose the kingdom, there is no indication that Jesus wanted people to sit back and wait for God to get the job done. Clearly, the teachings that we have discussed so far emphasize human responsibility and action. If this prayer is to be granted, we have a lot of work to do!

16

Unity in Action

"The Father and I are one."
John 10:30

Once again we encounter a statement that has been uniquely preserved in the Gospel of John. Given the dramatic claim that Jesus is making – identifying himself with God – many scholars, including me, do not think Jesus said these words. They are markedly different from the Synoptic Gospels' teachings of Jesus, which focus on social behaviour and depictions of the kingdom of God, as we saw in the previous chapter. But even though it may not have come from the historical Jesus, this statement has great significance within the Christian tradition.

The teaching appears in the context of one of a series of exchanges Jesus has with "the Jews" in the Gospel of John. Often, throughout this gospel, the phrase "the Jews" refers to people who do not believe in Jesus and are opposed to him. Such use of the phrase has had disastrous consequences for Christian–Jewish relations over the centuries, for it has contributed to Christian notions that "the Jews" are responsible for the death of Jesus, notions that are not true historically. As a result the world has witnessed a long history of Christian anti-Semitism, which led to ill-treatment of Jews in society and fuelled horrific violence towards Jews, including pogroms and the Holocaust. The author of the Gospel of John, however, who was likely a Jew, may be using this phrase simply as a way of identifying a group that is opposed to his or her group of Jews who do believe that Jesus is the Messiah. Thus, the intent of the phrase was not to promote anti-Semitism, but to distance the author's community from other groups that had different beliefs. In fact, many think that the Gospel of John was produced by a group of Jews who had been expelled from the synagogue because they accepted Jesus as the Messiah. This rejection by the synagogue may have led them to vilify those who had excluded them for their beliefs and to focus the gospel on the key contentious issue: the identity of Jesus.

The story that leads up to this statement depicts Jesus walking in the Jerusalem temple precincts during the Jewish Feast of Dedication. "The Jews" pressure him to tell them who he is. Is he the Messiah? Jesus does not answer directly, but instead stresses that the works he has done in God's name give testimony to him. He says that his sheep follow him, that he gives his followers eternal life, and that no one will take them from him. After he points out that what his Father has given him is greater than all else, the famous words appear: "The Father and I are one." This statement provokes "the Jews" to gather rocks to stone him, but Jesus protests, asking them for what noble work they are going to kill him. They claim that they want to destroy him for blaspheming, and Jesus responds with a short speech culminating in an exhortation for them to believe in his works so that they might "know and understand that the Father is in me and I am in the Father" (John 10:38). They try to arrest Jesus at this point, but he slips away from them.

What is particularly interesting about John 10:30 is that the Gospel does not use the expected term "messiah," but says that God and Jesus "are one." What does this mean? There are clues earlier in the story. Jesus said in John 10:28 that his sheep have been given eternal life and that no one can snatch them from his hand. The following verse states that what his Father has given him is greater than all else, and "no one can snatch it out of the Father's hand." This parallel between no one snatching Jesus' sheep from him and no one snatching anything from the Father's hand leads Scripture scholar Raymond Brown S.S. to conclude that the unity of John 10:30 is "a unity of power and operation."[9] God and Jesus are one because they act in the same way. Jesus interacts with human beings just as God does.

In the fourth century CE, when Christian leaders developed some of the key doctrines of the Christian church, texts such as these were very important. Particularly relevant here is the doctrine of the Trinity, in which three persons – the

Father, the Son and the Holy Spirit – share one nature. This nature was understood in terms of how the three persons acted. It is helpful to think about the identification of the three persons in terms of what they do, rather than solely in terms of who or what they are, which is very difficult to understand. Thinking of their actions, on the other hand, enables us to consider their love for creation and their willingness to be a reassuring presence – two characteristics that are particularly evident throughout the Gospel of John.

17

On Anxiety

"Do not worry about your life …"
Matthew 6:25

In the contemporary Western world, nearly everyone can understand what it means to worry. Given how future oriented North American society is, we often worry about what will happen later. Will we have enough money for retirement? Will we be able to pay back our debts? Will we have a job two years from now? Our days are filled with anxiety.

In Jesus' day people also worried, but the culture was not future oriented. People were concerned about their needs for the day. Would they have enough food and drink? Would they have shelter and clothing? It is true that many in North American society, as well as innumerable people in other countries, face similar fears, but in the first century, these concerns were the norm. Jesus addresses these anxieties head on with a series of exhortations found in Matthew 6:25-34 and Luke 12:22-31.

The consistent theme throughout these teachings is that we need not worry about what we will eat or drink or wear, for God provides for even the birds of the air, which do not sow nor reap nor gather into barns. Moreover, Jesus asks his followers to consider the lilies of the field, flowers more beautiful than King Solomon clothed in all of his glory, yet which neither toil nor spin. If God clothes the natural world so beautifully, the flowers and grasses which are alive one day and thrown into the oven the next, how much more so does God clothe human beings.

Notice the imagery Jesus uses in these teachings. He focuses upon things of the natural world – flowers and birds. This suggests that many in his audience would have been people used to rural living, for whom agriculture was probably the primary way of life. This is not the language of the city but of the country. Although Jesus' social status is disputed, many in his audience were peasants. Their lives were very difficult. They were at the mercy of the landowners who, in exchange for their labour, would offer food, protection and perhaps a loan when necessary. The landowners were patrons and the peasants their clients. Unfortunately for the clients, this relationship of patronage could easily become exploitative; the client could be forced to work harder and harder, or even be evicted from the land and driven to a life of destitution. Thus, the worries about where the next meal would come from were very real for countless numbers of people.

With these teachings, and others throughout the Gospels, the image of God presented is that of a provider who does not exploit. God is portrayed as being the opposite of earthly landowners who try to squeeze the peasants dry. As a result, Jesus' listeners may have perceived that embedded within these teachings was a critique of the patronage system, and the larger imperial rule of Rome that kept it in place.

Many interpreters of Scripture argue that here Jesus is providing another glimpse of a kingdom or empire that offers an alternative to that of Rome. In this realm, the basics for life – food, drink and clothing – are given by God. God is reliable and generous. But does this mean that humans should simply sit back and rely upon the motto "The Lord will provide"? Not at all. In Matthew 6:33, Jesus exhorts the audience to "strive first for the kingdom." In other words, humans have a role to play, a responsibility, in the creation of the kingdom. They must seek the kingdom, "and these things will be given [to them] as well" (Matthew 6:33). The notion that we need not worry is based on the creation of a different kingdom, where the obsession with security and having enough to eat will disappear; this is a realm in which people will have enough, and thus will not need to worry. If food and clothing are distributed fairly, no one should lack for them.

This teaching, therefore, is consistent with previous teachings about the generosity and reliability of God, as well as with descriptions of the kingdom. Although this talk of another empire is often missed by modern readers, an ancient listener would have understood it to be a criticism of the current one. How, then, might we who live today think about God's kingdom as something to strive for on earth? What is it in the contemporary, Western-driven empire that oppresses so many people, causing them to worry about their food and water for the day? How much responsibility for this situation lies with the corporate empires of the world?

These are huge questions, and the solutions to the problems created by systemically unjust economic and political policies are complex and difficult. But it is precisely these sorts of questions and issues that those who want to follow Jesus are called to tackle. Jesus is profoundly concerned about the poor and marginalized people around him, and he is willing to challenge the social systems that cause so many to suffer. Christians today are called to do the same.

18

Speck and Log

"Why do you notice the speck in
your neighbour's eye, but do not
notice the log in your own eye?"
Matthew 7:3

This teaching appears in Matthew's Sermon on
the Mount and Luke's Sermon on the Plain, which
means it goes back to Q. We probably remember
this famous statement being used to remind us not
to criticize other people unfairly.

Earlier we encountered sayings of Jesus that
deliberately exaggerate, or offer extreme examples.
Their distinctiveness makes the listener stop and
think. This is the case here, as well: no one could
ever have a log in her or his eye. The person hear-
ing these words would recognize the irony of criticizing others while ignoring one's own faults. Thus
the saying forces the hearer to take a good look at
himself or herself and focus on self-correction, as
illustrated by Matthew 7:4-5. Only then can one
attempt to offer constructive criticism to the other
person (Matthew 7:5).

The hypocrisy of judging others without identifying one's own failings is a consistent theme in the teachings of Jesus. Just before the saying about the speck and the log, Matthew's gospel has Jesus exhorting his followers not to pass judgment so that they may not be judged (Matthew 7:1). Matthew and Luke both cluster this "anti-judging" teaching with the speck and log teaching; Q probably did, too. This scenario indicates that the early Christians associated these sayings with each other.

Reprimanding people for judging others without taking a good look at themselves is not unique to Jesus. One finds widespread support for this approach among other Jewish and Christian sources. In the Second Testament, Paul picks up on this theme in Romans 2:1-3 with regard to the judgment of God, and the letter of James sounds remarkably similar to Matthew 7:1-2 when it states, "So who, then, are you to judge your neighbour?" Jesus appears to have been echoing a common wisdom teaching of his day.

What would judging and criticizing others entail in the ancient world? As we have seen, it was much less individualistic than modern Western society. People at that time understood themselves in relation to larger groups, such as their extended family and village. Judgment involves stereotyping them. Labelling a person or a group could affect their status within the community and their ability to interact with others. In ancient times, this labelling often meant linking a person or group with those who were viewed negatively in society, such as tax collectors and prostitutes. If one was a member of a family or village that had a low honour rating, one could be labelled for life, with little hope of escaping the stigma attached to being born into a dishonourable kin group.

Jesus not only criticizes this type of labelling, he associates with people whom many viewed negatively. On more than one occasion, Jesus is described as eating with questionable people, such as tax collectors and sinners (Mark 2:16-17), and earned a bad reputation because of it (Luke 15:1-2). Given that such activity is consistent with other things Jesus said and did, he probably did eat with such people. He went beyond instructing people not to judge others; he embodied this teaching by sharing a meal with those whom society scorned.

We have a better understanding today of the harm that stereotyping people from a family, social class, town, profession, or country can cause. Labelling certain ethnic and religious groups as "terrorists," or people with addictions as "failures," is also harmful. Some of us have been victims of stereotyping, or have done it to others. Jesus not only teaches that stereotyping is wrong, he spends time with those who are repeatedly judged and labelled by others. He does not appear to be concerned about his own reputation, but is open about his association with those whom the rest of society despises. He not only wanted people to resist judging, he wanted them to get to know those whom they tended to label or dismiss automatically. By getting to know people, to understand and appreciate them, we become less likely to judge them.

As for the speck and the log, although Jesus tells us we must see the log in our own eye before attempting to take a speck out of another's, the fact remains that correcting others is a reasonable thing to do. Offering helpful criticism is different from judging. Jesus does not hold back from correcting others, especially his disciples. But this reproof is done to benefit those being corrected – not to label or insult them. This is the vital difference.

While judgment and stereotyping are ills for us to avoid, offering healthy criticism to our friends, neighbours and associates – after we have examined and tried to remedy our own failings – is essential if we are to deal honestly and justly with one another.

19

Living for Others

"Those who try to make their
life secure will lose it, but those
who lose their life will save it."
Luke 17:33

As we have seen, Jesus sometimes uses parody and hyperbolic examples. With this teaching, we are faced with a paradox, a statement that on the surface appears contradictory, yet is in fact true. Another example of this approach in the sayings of Jesus is the famous admonition to "Love your enemies" (Matthew 5:44; Luke 6:27) – paradoxical because people tend to hate their enemies. The statement does not make any sense, until we understand that Jesus is asking us to re-evaluate our entire perspective when it comes to friends and enemies.

Luke 17:33 is a paradox because it does not seem to make sense. How can we save our life by losing it? What's more, no further explanation is forthcoming. The fact that this teaching appears in different forms in all four gospels, sometimes more than once per gospel (six times in total), suggests to scholars that it was probably a free-floating saying that early Christians took up and inserted into their texts in places they considered appropriate.

The saying appears twice in Luke's gospel: once here in chapter 17, and once in chapter 9 (v. 24), where it is one of the conditions of discipleship. There, the gospel writer has added "for my sake" after "those who lose their life," effectively Christianizing the saying and making it focus on Jesus. Because the version of the teaching in chapter 17 does not include this element, it is understood to be more authentic. The author of Luke's gospel places it in chapter 17, in the context of warnings about the coming transformation of the world, or apocalypse. Such a context indicates how the gospel writer interpreted the saying: as related to the afterlife or world to come. Indeed, this may be, in a completely different context, comparable to what Plato meant when he described Socrates as teaching that good philosophers practised dying and were confident that when life was over they would secure many blessings.[10] This is not necessarily the way that Jesus intended the saying to be interpreted, however.

If we examine the saying on its own, apart from the apocalyptic setting of Luke 17, the teaching can be understood to be about life in the here and now. Those who try to cling to life, and who focus upon security and health and comfort, will ultimately not be in the kingdom; they will not have life. The kingdom requires that we rely on God and live for others, not primarily for ourselves. By living for others, in a trusting relationship with God as a generous benefactor, we are in the kingdom and have life.

Although he uses different words and images, the apostle Paul picks up on this emphasis on living for others in his letters. Paul was apocalyptic – he thought God would intervene and transform the world within his own lifetime (see 1 Thessalonians 4:13-18). But he still argued that even though this event was imminent, people had to care for one another and stop focusing on their own wants and needs. For example, 1 Corinthians contains Paul's beautiful composition on the primacy of love over all other things, including knowledge, faith and prophetic powers (1 Corinthians 13:1-3). "Love bears all things, believes all things, hopes all things, endures all things," says Paul (1 Corinthians 13:7). In 1 Thessalonians, Paul acknowledges the love that the Thessalonians have for one another when he writes, "For you yourselves have been taught by God to love one another; and indeed you do love all the brothers and sisters throughout Macedonia." He goes on to say, "But we urge you, beloved, to do so more and more ..." (1 Thessalonians 4:9-10). We could add more examples of this emphasis upon love from Paul's letters, but the point is clear: love for others is a central ethic of the emerging church. It is fair to say that for both Jesus and Paul, love is central to what it means to be alive. If we live primarily to protect our own life, we are not loving others, and thus we are not truly alive.

In our hurried, stressed society, people are often focused primarily on survival. The uncertainty of employment, the cost of living, intense competition – all these factors contribute to a kind of rat-race mentality that often leads people to focus on themselves, even at the expense of others. Even taking the time to offer hospitality is difficult for many. Many people can relate to the notion of loving others intensely, but only with family members or close friends. Notice that when Paul stresses love in his letters, however, he is referring to the larger community, such as all the peoples throughout Macedonia. In 1 Corinthians, the church is fraught with disagreement and conflict, so Paul urges love between them, knowing full well that the members come from different backgrounds and do not have the same social status. For Jesus and Paul, love is not reserved for certain people. For Jesus, especially, it is intended for the weakest in society.

Imagine if people today lived their lives focused on loving the stranger and the outcast. Many do, but imagine a mass love movement! It may sound crazy and idealistic, but if a majority of people, even in one single country, or one single city, decided to take up this banner, how different things could be. We have seen it manifest itself in some small communities, such as the Catholic Worker or other forms of communal living, so we know it can work and make sense. In these small pockets of love, we find hope that Jesus' teachings are viable.

20

Love for Friends

"No one has greater love
than this, to lay down one's
life for one's friends."
John 15:13

These words, found only in the Gospel of John, offer a concrete example of what it means to love another person. The teaching is embedded within Jesus' famous farewell discourse to his disciples, which he delivers before his arrest and crucifixion. He states a clear commandment: "Love one another, as I have loved you," then elaborates upon the greatest love, which is to lay down one's life for one's friends.

This teaching builds upon the old and rich tradition of friendship, one of the most idealized of relationships within the ancient world. Stories of great friends reach back at least as far as Homer, who narrates the exploits of Achilles and Patroclus; numerous subsequent philosophers and poets offer systematic and detailed reflection upon friendship. Although such stories are not as pervasive within Hebrew literature, the great friendship between David and Jonathan is described in 1 Samuel 18:1, and the Hellenistic Jewish wisdom of Sirach offers considerable advice about what a true friend is (Sirach 6:7-17).

The philosopher Aristotle has probably had the most impact upon theories and understandings of friendship within Greek thought. According to Aristotle, friendship is essential for happiness and, in its highest form, exists between people of good character.[11] Aristotle joins many later writers, including the author of the Gospel of John, in stressing that true friends should be willing to sacrifice their lives for one another.[12]

Vocabulary and ideas associated with this ideal can be found in other early Christian texts as well. In the Acts of the Apostles, for example, the early Christian community is depicted as sharing all things in common (Acts 2:44; 4:32), a feature of friendship that reputedly originated with Pythagoras.[13] Paul uses the language of friendship when he speaks of sharing "one soul" with the Philippians (Philippians 1:27). Being of "one soul" or "one mind" is a typical feature of friendship within Greek literature. Some consider Philippians to be a friendship letter. The letter of James uses typical friendship motifs. It calls Abraham a "friend of God" (James 2:23), a description found in other Jewish texts, and stresses that "friendship with the world is enmity with God" (James 4:4). As we can see, themes and vocabulary associated with the rich tradition of friendship in the ancient world easily make their way into the literature of early Christianity.

In John's Gospel, the notion of laying down one's life for one's friends is important for the community that produced and used this text. It is this type of behaviour that is expected of the Good Shepherd in John 10:11, 15, 17-18. In a later letter that may come from the same community, members of the group must be willing to die for one another (1 John 3:16). This emphasis upon loving one another is different from the commandment to "love your enemies." It may have grown out of the community's sense of alienation from the larger synagogue and possible fear of persecution, a persecution that could have required that members die for one another. Even though the radical "love your enemies" is not present in the teaching in John 15, this courage needed to be ready to die for one another is not to be underestimated.

The language of friendship continues in this gospel when Jesus tells his disciples that they are his friends if they do as he commands. No longer does he call them servants, but friends "because I have made known to you everything that I have heard from my Father" (John 15:15). Jesus' followers are called his friends (the Greek word is *philoi*) because they also possess the wisdom that has been given to Jesus by God. Such an idea recalls a passage in the Wisdom of Solomon that states, "In every generation [wisdom] passes into holy souls and makes them friends of God and prophets; for God loves nothing so much as the person who lives with wisdom" (Wisdom of Solomon 7:27-28). The gift of wisdom is central to both texts – in generating friendship with Jesus or friendship with God.

The exchange of frank criticism was another typical feature of ancient friendship. We may find it difficult to offer this kind of criticism to our friends, for fear they will resent it. But criticism that is directly honest is often so refreshing!

Friendship is surely an important type of relationship today, although we may treat it more superficially in modern Western society. We may refer to people as friends, but would we die for them? Would we be willing to suffer for them if necessary? Would we bear with them and remain loyal, even if it meant losing respect and honour in other people's eyes? Whether it is through texts such as the Gospel of John, or others, people today have much to learn from descriptions of this ancient ideal.

21

God and the Emperor

"Give to the emperor the things
that are the emperor's, and to
God the things that are God's."
Mark 12:17

In the opening chapter, I briefly described the political context of first-century Palestine. Given that Jesus directly refers to the emperor, meaning the Roman emperor, in this teaching, it is appropriate to say a little more about the nature of the Roman empire at that time.

As we saw earlier, by the time of Jesus, Rome had become the imperial power throughout the Mediterranean. In 63 BCE, under General Pompey, Rome had conquered the region of Palestine, which included Galilee and Judea among other provinces. Thereafter, the region was administered through client kings and the Jewish high priesthood. Although Rome did not rule directly, it still reaped the benefits of its territorial expansion, integrating Palestine into its overall economic machine. Peasants and others living in the area began to pay tribute to Rome, as well as to the local ruler, such as Herod the Great, on top of the temple tax for the Jerusalem temple. In addition, the fruits of the harvests throughout the empire were now used to feed people in the city of Rome, which had grown to a huge size. Not surprisingly, the typical Palestinian had little sympathy for Caesar.

Rome tended to assert its power through terror. If a local rebellion sprang up, the military would quash it immediately, often burning entire villages, as it did in the rebellion of 4 BCE (around the time Jesus was born). According to the Jewish historian Josephus, the Romans reputedly crucified over two thousand people during this uprising.[14] Crucifixion was an excruciatingly painful form of execution, usually reserved for upstart slaves or rebellious bandits, and highly effective in spreading dread among the populace. One of the very worst instances of Roman power and terror was during the Jewish revolt of 66–70 CE, when some Jews rose up against Roman domination. The Romans besieged the city of Jerusalem, burning it, destroying the temple, and killing thousands of people in the streets. Josephus describes the horror, claiming that as poor Jerusalemites fled the city, the armies caught them and tortured them, crucifying them in all sorts of positions for the soldiers' amusement.[15]

The people had good reason to resent Roman rule as well as the rule of the local leaders, many of whom built lavish houses and fortresses at the expense of the local peasants. Although these peasants had lived under one empire after another for many years, Rome, especially its military force, had introduced an oppression of unparalleled power and terror.

Here is the context of the "Give to the emperor" saying in the Gospel of Mark: some Pharisees and Herodians were sent to Jesus to trap him with a question. They ask if it is lawful to pay taxes to the emperor? Jesus, realizing that they are trying to trap him, requests a coin. He examines it, then asks whose picture and name are on it. They respond, "The emperor's." Jesus then makes the famous statement: "Give to the emperor the things that are the emperor's, and to God the things that are God's." His listeners are amazed.

It is impossible to know for sure the historical context of this teaching, for in other ancient sources, such as the gospel of Thomas (Thomas 100:1-4), the context is different. The teaching itself, however, remains essentially the same in all of the Gospels in which it is preserved (Mark, Matthew and Luke). Regardless of what question may have been posed to Jesus (presumably it had something to do with paying taxes to Caesar), he provides a clever response. He does not answer the question directly; he does not tell his audience what to do. Rather, as is typical in many of his teachings, he makes a general statement that causes his listeners to think. In this case, it might provoke them to ask, "Well, what does belong to Caesar and what belongs to God?"

In the first century, religion and politics were not separate from one another. For Jews, everything belonged to God, their creator. The notion that a certain quantifiable amount of things belonged to Caesar, even though he was worshipped as a god and saviour by many, made no sense. Although Jews could be tortured and killed by the Romans for refusing to pay tribute to Caesar, according to Jewish law it was illegal to pay such monies to Rome. While Jesus does not fall into the trap of answering a question about taxes directly, Jews who are listening to him would realize that he is reminding them that nothing belongs to Caesar; all belongs to God! As biblical scholar Richard Horsley states, "Jesus is clearly and simply reasserting the Israelite principle that Caesar, or any other imperial ruler, has no claim on the Israelite people, since God is their actual king and master."[16]

We in the West live in a very different context than that of the Roman empire, even though imperialism and exploitation continue to run rampant. Democracy, despite its faults and foibles, is seen by many to be one of the best ways of organizing societies that are highly diverse with regard to religion, ethnicity, and culture, and of maximizing the number of voices that can be heard. According to Jesus, the kingdom of God welcomes the poor, the sick and the marginalized. I therefore suggest that this teaching, despite its implicit criticism of the political context of its day, does not mean that the state is bad or should be abandoned. Rather, I think Jesus would likely promote an organization of power wherein the poor were cared for and people could be directly involved in determining their future. No doubt Jesus would be extremely critical of many current political leaders and their governments that act irresponsibly, rashly and oppressively, but it would be wrong to say that he was against all government at all times. Perhaps he would reserve the most contempt today for giant corporations and their shareholders, whose purpose is to make a profit despite the effect on humanity and the planet. What makes these entities somewhat forbidding is that their leaders are not elected; they answer primarily to their shareholders, for whom they must make money. We are all aware of the various types of exploitation, of human beings and of the earth, that such companies have committed. If we want to take Jesus' teaching seriously, then we must not only insist that our governments be accountable and fair in determining how wealth is distributed, but that corporate powers be made accountable as well.

22

Honour, Shame and the Kingdom

"For there are eunuchs who
have been so from birth, and
there are eunuchs who have been
made eunuchs by others, and there
are eunuchs who have made themselves eunuchs for the sake of the
kingdom of heaven."
Matthew 19:12

This teaching is unique to the Gospel of Matthew. The writer, who places it after Jesus' teachings on divorce, introduces it by having Jesus say that not everyone can accept the teaching, "only those to whom it has been given" (Matthew 19:12), and concludes with "Let anyone accept this who can" (Matthew 19:12). The gospel writer likely added this framing because the teaching is difficult to understand, and is not something that every male can uphold.

A eunuch is a castrated male (the testicles are crushed or removed). As the teaching illustrates, this castration can occur in one of three ways: the man is born that way, has been castrated by others, or has castrated himself. Slaves who worked in royal households were often castrated so they would not pose any sexual threat to the women. Some free men were castrated in order to publicly humiliate them. Males who were born eunuchs or made that way by others were forbidden from the temple service because they were not complete and could not father children, as males were expected to do. This ban against eunuchs was upheld by the Jewish Law. For example, Deuteronomy 23:1 states, "No one whose testicles are crushed or whose penis is cut off shall be admitted to the assembly of the Lord." In sum, to be a eunuch meant that one had not only physical limitations, but social and religious restrictions as well.

In a society that had an honour/shame code, eunuchs were perceived as highly dishonourable, for the testicles were the symbol of male honour. They stood for manliness, authority over family, and courage and strength in opposing threats from others. Women's shame was symbolized by the hymen, which stood for the female virtues of timidity, control, modesty and quietness. Sirach 25–26 provides descriptions of various types of wives, stating, for example, that "A silent wife is a gift from the Lord, and nothing is so precious as her self-discipline" (Sirach 26:14). Gender roles were clear and restrictive. If a man acted in an effeminate manner or a woman behaved aggressively, he or she violated the whole code of honour and shame and the power configurations that this code supported. Moreover, because the male eunuch's physical difference was permanent, he was forever condemned to be ridiculed and excluded. This meant a life on the margins of society.

This teaching can be understood, therefore, as another criticism by Jesus of the structural injustices created by a male-dominated and patriarchal society – if not an outright attack against it. Eunuchs, like women, children, the sick and the poor, suffered in such a society. By saying that some men make themselves eunuchs for the sake of the kingdom, Jesus is suggesting that some are willing to withstand the dishonour such an identity would entail. Perhaps one could go further and say that the kingdom will not uphold the values of honour and shame. In the kingdom, it will not matter if one is a eunuch or not, because people will not be forced to fit into a prescribed gender role. Males will not have to project a tough, powerful persona in the kingdom, nor will females have to behave shyly, quietly and modestly. By showing support for eunuchs, Jesus is effectively undermining some of the cultural and social values at the heart of his society and offering another glimpse of what the kingdom will be like.

In the past, many have understood this teaching to mean that Jesus is advocating celibacy, and it was used in such a way in the early church. It is said that the Christian biblical scholar and theologian Origen (ca. 185–253 CE) castrated himself under the influence of this teaching. Today, however, few scholars think that Jesus taught others to be celibate. Rather, this teaching is consistent with many others that we have discussed. It challenges the honour/shame game and forces people to think differently about the social codes they had lived with all their lives. It supports an especially humiliated marginal group – eunuchs – and thereby undermines the stress put on male honour.

Although the gender roles of contemporary North American culture are not as rigid as those of first-century Palestine, such roles are still very much at work, and still marginalize people. Many men and women suffer psychologically and emotionally when they do not fulfill cultural and family expectations, whether that means marrying, having children, pursuing "appropriate" employment or behaving in a "ladylike" or "manly" fashion. Obviously, the discrimination against gays and lesbians is relevant here, for many understand homosexuality as a violation of the way things are supposed to be. Gender roles seem to be one of the hardest patterns and sets of values to challenge, for they undergird a whole system of power relations and are profoundly ingrained in many people from the day they are born. Some individuals do not want to discuss alternatives to how men and women should act, or how families should be structured; to think about this question can be disturbing at a deep emotional level. Yet by offering this teaching, Jesus is willing to challenge entrenched values. Are we willing to engage in similar challenges today?

23

Family and Discipleship

"Whoever comes to me and
does not hate father and mother,
wife and children, brothers and
sisters, yes, and even life itself,
cannot be my disciple."
Luke 14:26

The importance of kinship and family ties for first-century Mediterranean people has been asserted several times throughout this book. There is no question that in ancient societies, as in many societies today, one's family was central to one's identity and livelihood. Those without a family, such as widows and orphans, were among the weakest and most vulnerable in society as they had no one to support them. If a family member was dishonoured, the entire family experienced dishonour. People understood themselves in relation to the rest of their family, and others perceived them as belonging to a particular family first, and as an individual second.

It is easy to imagine that the teaching here would not go over well with many of Jesus' listeners. In fact, some of the parallels to the saying in other gospels, such as the Gospel of Matthew (Matthew 10:37), soften the teaching to say: "Whoever loves father or mother more than me is not worthy of me; and whoever loves son or daughter more than me is not worthy of me." Matthew, presumably to make the saying more palatable to his audience, stresses that people should not love their family members "more" than they love Jesus.

Luke, however, uses "hate" – a strong word. We tend to associate hatred with vindictiveness, but in ancient Greek, this word could also connote renunciation. Thus Jesus is probably not telling people to hate their family in the sense of wishing them dead or wanting them to suffer; rather, disciples must be willing to renounce and forsake family in order to follow Jesus.

Jesus' insistence that his followers must be ready to give up family in order to follow him appears elsewhere in the gospel. Luke 9:57-62 contains a couple of teachings indicating that Jesus and his followers do not have a permanent home, but travel around – like the Cynics we encountered earlier – with no place to call their own. Evidence of this itinerant lifestyle is provided when a person vows that he will follow Jesus wherever he goes, and Jesus responds, "Foxes have holes, and birds of the air have nests; but the Son of Man has nowhere to lay his head " (Luke 9:57-58). Subsequently, Jesus tells another to follow him; the man asks to first go and bury his dead father, a proper burial being a primary obligation of children to their parents. Jesus' reply is shocking: "Let the dead bury their own dead; but as for you, go and proclaim the kingdom of God" (Luke 9:59-60). When a third person says he will follow Jesus, but first wants to say goodbye to those at his home, again Jesus warns, "No one who puts a hand to the plow and looks back is fit for the kingdom of God" (Luke 9:61-62). Clearly, biological ties to family were not Jesus' top priority.

There is no indication that Jesus thought family was a bad thing in itself, for some stories attributed to him, such as the parable of the Prodigal Son (Luke 15:11-32), celebrate family reconciliation. But a culture that puts too much emphasis on family ties can easily marginalize those who are without familial relationships. Giving so much importance to family can become another form of idolatry. Jesus, as we know, ate with all kinds of people, including sinners, and often featured sick people, widows, day labourers and children in his teachings and parables. He did not focus upon his own biological family and, in fact, seemed to be creating a new family that was not based upon biological ties. For Jesus, our primary loyalty should not be to the family, but to God and the kingdom.

Many concur that a solid family is the foundation of society. Yet many today do not have a family; the primacy of the biological family can continue to cause suffering if it does not look beyond itself to include others. Jesus' emphasis upon things greater than the family, such as the kingdom, and his welcoming of all types of people into his family is important. It reminds us that we all have an obligation to the larger human family, which includes people of all ethnicities, religions and social classes. By caring for all our brothers and sisters, not just our biological ones, we live out Jesus' teachings.

24

A Kingdom Among You

> "The kingdom of God is not
> coming with things that can be
> observed; nor will they say, 'Look,
> here it is!' or 'There it is!' For, in fact,
> the kingdom of God is among you."
> Luke 17:20-21

Many apocalyptic groups existed in antiquity. The Jews who produced the Dead Sea Scrolls, for example, expected God to intervene and save the righteous and destroy the wicked. John the Baptist preached an apocalyptic message (see Matthew 3:11-12; Luke 3:15-18). We have seen how Paul anticipated a transformation in his own lifetime. This is especially clear in 1 Thessalonians, where he states that although the Lord will return without warning, "like a thief in the night" (1 Thessalonians 5:2), "we who are alive, who are left, will be caught up in the clouds together with them [those who have already died] to meet the Lord in the air; and so we will be with the Lord forever" (1 Thessalonians 4:17). Incidentally, the latter text was used as a "proof text" for the invention of something called "The Rapture" – the notion that somehow members of the church will be "raptured" or taken up to be with Jesus while the earth experiences a great tribulation – devised by a nineteenth-century minister named John Nelson Darby. However, 1 Thessalonians gives no indication that Christians will be gathered into a "safe zone" while havoc is wreaked on the earth.

The most apocalyptic text in the Second Testament is the Book of Revelation, or the Apocalypse of John, which depicts the visions of one John of Patmos. These visions detail all sorts of disasters and catastrophes that befall those who are perceived to be opposed to Christ (e.g., Revelation 9:13-19). Several figures in these visions are thought to be symbolic of earthly rulers and powers, including Rome and the Roman emperor (e.g., Revelation 13:11-18). Thus, many understand the book of Revelation to be a highly political text that uses all sorts of apocalyptic imagery in an attempt to cry out against the powers and forces that were persecuting the early Christians.

Although some streams of the early church continued to believe and proclaim these apocalyptic traditions, it is highly disputed whether Jesus was an apocalyptic Jew. Apocalyptic proclamations, such as those found in Mark 13, have been attributed to him, but many scholars think the gospel writers put those words on Jesus' lips because they reflected what the church believed. Although space does not permit me to explore all the reasons why I do not think Jesus was apocalyptic, this teaching from Luke's gospel (and the Gospel of Thomas 113:1-2) strongly suggests that he was not.

In Luke, this teaching is a response to some Pharisees who ask when the kingdom of God is coming. Jesus makes it clear that the kingdom cannot be predicted with signs or observable things; the kingdom is among human society and is already present. Such an idea is buttressed by the version in the Gospel of Thomas, in which Jesus says that the kingdom is spread out upon the earth, and people do not see it. Luke 11:20, where Jesus says, "But if it is by the finger of God that I cast out demons, then the kingdom of God has come to you," also seems to support this non-apocalyptic view. Despite the apocalyptic traditions associated with Jesus, clear glimpses in the tradition (other teachings and parables would also support this "kingdom is now" perspective) support another perspective.

Although we often dismiss tabloid magazines' latest headlines announcing that the world will end in six days, or that so-and-so is the anti-Christ, it is important to be aware that apocalyptic thinking, in its tremendous variety of forms and degrees of intensity, is powerful in the world today in many religions, especially Christianity. Just think of the *Left Behind* series of books, which have become bestsellers and are sold in bookstores everywhere.[17] This type of theology has a significant impact, for some apocalypticists equate conflicts and events in the world with biblical stories and apocalyptic visions, as if everything that is happening was somehow destined by God.

In my view, this is dangerous thinking, for it can easily lead humans to give up their responsibility to try to create a better world because they think that God will step in and bring some sort of transformation or set everything straight. Such an attitude seems a far cry from the message of Jesus, who is constantly exhorting people to do good; to practise economic and social justice; and to love others, including our enemies.

25

Memory

"Do this in remembrance of me."
Luke 22:19

The way we remember Jesus matters. It matters because the memory of Jesus is significant for many Christians as they struggle to determine how they should live and what their priorities should be. Not surprisingly then, the debate about who Jesus was historically, and what he taught, can be intense.

As we have seen at various points in this book, the majority of biblical scholars do not think that many teachings and stories associated with Jesus in the gospels emerged from the historical Jesus. Rather, these grew out of the early Christian traditions that developed soon after his death. Just because these teachings and stories may not come from Jesus, however, does not mean that they are not important or meaningful. On the contrary, they offer insight on how the early church was developing and manifest a deep wisdom that can inform people's thinking.

"Do this in remembrance of me" is a teaching that appears during the Last Supper scene in the Gospel of Luke. Matthew and Mark include similar scenes but do not contain these words, and there is no meal in the Gospel of John. Although many scholars think it is almost impossible to know exactly what Jesus said at this meal, these words play a significant and powerful role in the Christian tradition, for they point to the importance of doing and remembering. It is significant that when Paul instructs the Corinthians about how they should celebrate the Lord's Supper, he uses these very words (1 Corinthians 11:23-25). For Paul, this supper is central to the Christian community, for in its celebration, the community is articulating and practising the heart of what they believe. If this supper is taken amidst factionalism in the church, or if the wealthier members of the church eat before poorer ones are able to get there, then Paul thinks that such a meal is useless and is not a celebration of the Lord's supper at all (1 Corinthians 11:20).

The point of Paul's teaching here is that if we truly want to remember Jesus, then we do so by the way we live! We have seen throughout this book that how we live and treat others is at the heart of Jesus' teaching. The kingdom is not something that will arrive on clouds, but happens, in part, through our actions. Although Paul and many early Christians move in the direction of apocalypticism, they are still firmly focused upon treating one another out of love. It is through such loving action – not quarrelling, boasting, or eloquent wisdom (1 Corinthians 1:17) – that we remember Jesus.

I hope that my interpretation of some of Jesus' teachings in this short study will prompt you to explore these teachings more fully and to grapple with the difficult task of thinking about how such teachings can inform our world today. Although we must keep in mind that the message of Jesus and the Second Testament writers comes from a very different place, time, and culture, these teachings can help us re-examine and challenge contemporary practice. They are central to the Christian tradition. Equipped with our reason and experience, as well as the accumulated wisdom of the centuries, we can continue to engage these teachings and keep the memory of Jesus alive.

Notes

[1] The Gospel of Thomas contains teachings of Jesus, some of which find parallels in Matthew, Mark and Luke. This Gospel was discovered in 1945, in Nag Hammadi, Egypt.

[2] John Dominic Crossan, *The Historical Jesus: The Life of a Mediterranean Jewish Peasant* (San Francisco: Harper, 1991), 266–74.

[3] Jerome, *In Hieremiam* 2.5.2.

[4] Bruce J. Malina and Richard L. Rohrbaugh, *Social Science Commentary on the Synoptic Gospels* (Minneapolis: Fortress, 1992), 324.

[5] Crossan, *The Historical Jesus*, 266–74.

[6] Muriel Lester, "Tale from Vienna," in Walter Wink, ed., *Peace is the Way: Writings on Nonviolence from the Fellowship of Reconciliation* (Maryknoll, NY: Orbis, 2000), 260–61.

[7] W.H. Auden, *Selected Poems* (London: Faber and Faber, 1979), 7.

[8] Pseudo-Diogenes *Epistle*, 11.

[9] Raymond E. Brown, S.S. *The Gospel According to John I–XII* (AB 29; New York: Doubleday) 407.

[10] Plato, *Phaedo* 64A.

[11] Aristotle, *Nichomachean Ethics* 8.3.6.

[12] Aristotle, *Nichomachean Ethics* 9.8.3.

[13] Diogenes Laertius, *Lives* 8.10.

[14] Josephus, *War* 2. 71–76.

[15] Josephus, *War* 7. 132–55.

[16] Richard A. Horsley, *Jesus and Empire: The Kingdom of God and the New World Disorder* (Minneapolis: Fortress, 2003), 99.

[17] The *Left Behind* series, by Tim LaHaye and Jerry B. Jenkins, has sold over 50 million copies in the United States alone. Although the series is fictional, many people in the US take it quite seriously.

Index of Scripture References

Other books in the
Jesus Speaks Today series

The Questions of Jesus
JOHN L. McLAUGHLIN

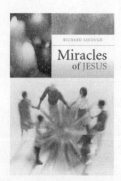